MAY 0 3 2006

TEACHING
Self-Discipline

For Self-Reliance and Academic Success

Dennis Knapczyk

IEP RESOURCES

CMC
153.8
K726t
2004

WITHDRAWN

N.C. WESLEYAN COLLEGE
ELIZABETH BRASWELL PEARSALL LIBRARY

Teaching Self-Discipline Win/Mac CD

The CD provided contains a printable PDF file of this entire book.
You can review and print pages from your computer.
The PDF (portable document format) file requires **Acrobat Reader** software.

• If you have **Acrobat Reader** already on your computer,
run the program and then open the file Using **TEACHself.pdf** from the CD.

• **To Install Acrobat Reader for Windows**: Run **ARINSTALL.EXE** provided on the CD.
After installation, run Acrobat Reader then open using TEACHself.pdf

• **To install Acrobat Reader for Mac**: Run **Reader Installer**.
After installation, open using **TEACHself.pdf**

Author: Dennis Knapczyk
Editor: Tom Kinney
Graphic Design: Sherry Pribbenow

An Attainment Publication

©2004 Attainment Company, Inc. All Rights Reserved.
Printed in the United States of America.

ISBN 1-57861-525-9

P.O. Box 930160
Verona, Wisconsin   53593-0160
Phone 800-327-4269   Fax 800.942.3865

www.AttainmentCompany.com

Table of Contents

Acknowledgements and Dedication

We are led to believe that self-discipline is something innate or inherent in the individual and that something is fundamentally wrong with those who lack self-discipline. This book is dedicated to all the children and youth who have shown me that self-discipline is actually something we all learn and that what is "wrong" with those who seem undisciplined is their not learning the proper skills to negotiate their behavior. To you, I extend my heartfelt wish that this book will help your teachers and caregivers in teaching you the skills for becoming more self-reliant and disciplined. To Paul Rodes who helped with the conceptual frame work. And to my wife Susan and to my children who have shown patience and support for my work.

About the Author

Dennis Knapczyk is Professor of Education and Director of the Collaborative Teacher Education Program (CTEP) at Indiana University on the Bloomington campus. He started teaching back in 1966 as a teacher's aid at Fairview State Hospital in Costa Mesa, California. He received his teacher's license and master's degree at what is now California State University at Fullerton, and from 1967 to 1969 he was a special education teacher at Trident Junior High School in Anaheim, California. In 1972, he received his PhD. from Kansas University and started working as a university professor and teacher educator at Indiana University in Bloomington. In 1985, he started the Collaborative Teacher Education Program, which is still in operation today. CTEP is a graduate level program that has used a variety of distance education technologies to offer certification coursework to in-service special education teachers in Central and Southern Indiana. His areas of research and teaching include social skills instruction, classroom and behavior management, curriculum development and assessment, instructional design and distance education. He has a wife and five children, runs a tree farm, does woodworking, and loves to jog, bicycle, hike, camp and canoe.

Introduction

Discipline is viewed by many teachers as a necessary evil — something they have to do in order to create an atmosphere in which to teach. Rarely is it thought of as an actual instructional area. In Teaching Self-Discipline we will look at classroom discipline as a curricular concern, comparable to teaching reading, math and the other instructional areas. Rather than presenting discipline as something teachers do to students, you will learn that it is something you can teach them to do themselves.

Typically, students learn self-discipline throughout their schooling. They learn to do such things as:

— Set goals and priorities for their behavior.

— Delay gratification of desired outcomes.

— Apply themselves to their work.

— Direct their behavior into acceptable channels.

— Make judgments and decisions about their actions.

— Moderate their actions in accordance with the demands of teachers and peers.

Thus, while self-discipline is an important part of what students learn in school, many approaches to discipline overlook this fact. Instead their focus is mainly on teacher-directed managing of students rather than on student learning. If we see discipline as an instructional issue, we begin to understand that our real aim is not getting students to behave, but to teach them to take responsibility for their own behavior.

In Teaching Self-Discipline you will learn how to help your students develop the skills to manage and regulate their behavior more effectively, and to use methods for teaching and reinforcing key self-discipline skills. The book describes the process of teaching and supporting self-discipline both with individual students and with groups. It addresses the most immediate and pressing needs of teachers, and also provides a framework for developing long-

"Discipline is viewed by many teachers as a necessary evil — something they have to do in order to create an atmosphere in which to teach. Rarely is it thought of as an actual instructional area."

range goals and lessons. It does not, however, attempt to show you how to address more serious and long-standing problems that may require clinical or systematic approaches, such as counseling, therapy or behavior management.

Teaching Self-discipline begins by introducing the concept of self-discipline and showing how it can be viewed as a curriculum content area.

Chapter One — explains how approaches to classroom discipline can be redirected toward teaching students to manage their own behavior and discusses how self-discipline skills are crucial to student behavior in three areas: Managing performance, managing motivation and managing judgments.

Chapter Two — shows how to turn problems of student discipline into self-discipline goals on which to focus your teaching. The next three chapters are devoted to the important skill areas pertaining to self-discipline.

Chapter Three — focuses on managing performance or the series of actions students must manage to complete tasks and activities successfully.

Chapter Four — centers on managing motivation which is the driving force for student behavior that comes from the results and outcomes of successful performance.

Chapter Five — discusses managing judgments which are the decisions about behavior that enable students to effectively adjust and regulate their behavior. Each of these chapters shows how to identify the instructional needs students may have in the skill area and presents a wide variety of teaching methods for addressing these needs.

Chapter Six — explains how to plan and monitor lessons for teaching self-discipline so you can integrate this area of instruction in your everyday teaching schedule and routine. The last two chapters show how to help students combine and extend their self-discipline skills to achieve higher levels of independence and self-direction.

Chapter Seven — discusses managing habits which are the building blocks of efficient, productive behavior.

Chapter Eight — focuses on ways to encourage students to take ownership and responsibility for achieving school goals and to take initiative in pursuing their personal aims and interests. Many of the chapters also contain worksheets and case study examples to guide your planning and teaching.

Chapter 1

Thinking About Self-Discipline and Observing Student Behavior

The Nature of Self-Discipline

Every teacher realizes that discipline is important in school. When the topic comes up, teachers immediately think of students like Ramon, who talks out in class; Tanika, who is always out of her seat; Julie, who doesn't get her work done; or Orville, who simply can't seem to control himself. The challenges involved in teaching students like these often have less to do with specific academic skills like reading, doing math computation or remembering spelling words than they do with getting these students to demonstrate the motivation, concentration, and self-control that will make their studies successful. When asked about the problems they face in their classes, most teachers will answer by describing the difficulties they have with controlling student behavior and encouraging active participation, rather than with teaching academic tasks.

But while teachers are readily aware of discipline problems among their students, it's less common for them to consider the real nature of self-discipline — the proficient, capable behavior that most students use to be successful in school. Every day, students apply themselves to their work, moderate their actions in accordance with the demands of teachers and peers, postpone gratification of desired outcomes, and engage in a host of other behaviors that allow them to direct and control their actions so they can make the most of learning opportunities. Because self-discipline is learned more or less incidentally, rather than through deliberate curricular instruction, we often fail to recognize how remarkable and complex it is. This chapter will give an overview of some of the important features of self-discipline, and it will offer a framework for observing and thinking about this area of behavior in your school settings.

"While teachers are readily aware of discipline problems among their students, it's less common for them to consider the real nature of self-discipline – the proficient, capable behavior that most students use to be successful in school."

Self-Discipline is an Integral Part of all School Settings

Self-discipline is the ability to take responsibility and ownership for one's behavior, and it encompasses many of the actions, decisions and judgments students go through every day in school. We teachers often think of school demands in fairly simple and concrete terms: paying attention in class, making comments in a discussion, talking with friends in the cafeteria, filling in answers on a worksheet. But demands like these actually represent a considerable range of behavior that students must learn to negotiate proficiently. To perform well in school, students must be able to moderate and shape their behavior to fit changing circumstances, to judge the effects of what they do, and to determine the proper times and places to display their actions. They must also be able to persevere in their behavior, weigh alternative ends, track progress toward desired outcomes and draw incentive from both the immediate and the long term results of their performance.

Self-Discipline Requires Discrete Skills

Self-discipline involves specific skills that students must learn to use in a particular situation. These skills enable students to establish clear, precise goals for their actions, aid them in keeping a fixed purpose and direction in mind while doing these actions, and help them to evaluate their behavior and make future plans after performance has taken place. For example, when we have students work together on a small group project, we are actually asking them to plan and coordinate a considerable range of skilled behavior that includes:

— transforming our directions into a group plan for completing required tasks and sub-tasks,

— deciding on an effective approach for carrying out the necessary activities,

— establishing a division of labor in the group for performing the tasks and sub-tasks,

— building rapport among group members by chatting, smiling, and encouraging one another,

— negotiating differences of opinion and achieving consensus on how to accomplish tasks,

— supporting one another's work, such as by helping a group member understand how to complete specific tasks,

— monitoring the completion of tasks, and comparing the group's accomplishments with the teacher's expectations.

> "Self-discipline is the ability to take responsibility and ownership for one's behavior."

At the same time, students have to delay or control personal desires and impulses and make judgments about such issues as the rate and quality of their work, their position and standing in the group, and overall group atmosphere.

In the same way, non-academic situations such as talking with friends during lunchtime or playing on the playground also require a complex range of skills. Although we often think of such activities as fairly loose and free of form, they often include demands that are even more subtle and sophisticated than those students meet in class. When students have conversations in the cafeteria, for example, they are actually coordinating a notable range of behavior:

— listening to others when they speak,

— formulating relevant comments quickly,

— keeping up with changes or shifts in the conversation,

— drawing on background knowledge to comment on popular subjects,

— evaluating the mood and prevailing opinion of the group before speaking,

— recognizing conversational taboos and limits,

— using body language to show interest, convey emotions and build rapport,

— formulating strategies to impress friends or enhance status with group members,

— deferring to the more popular students or to group leaders,

— controlling or masking personal feelings about individual group members and their opinions.

Thus in classrooms, the lunchroom and every other school setting, students use self-discipline to meet prevailing demands in a reasonably measured and consistent manner. The skills for self-discipline help students plan and coordinate their actions, keep track of the outcomes or rewards for their performance, and judge how their actions fit in with what is going on around them. These skills allow students to control their own behavior and to generate the motivation and willingness to perform in prescribed ways.

Self-Discipline as an Aim of Instruction

As the above description indicates, self-discipline has much in common with classroom discipline or management practices, but it encompasses these areas as they are manifested in student behavior rather than teacher behavior. It extends beyond what teachers may do to motivate, control and discipline students and it centers on the logical aim toward which such practices should be directed. That is, self-discipline is ultimately exercised independently of teachers, peers or any other source of external assistance. It is something students do for themselves and for their own set of reasons. Thus, teaching self-discipline involves showing students how to manage their own actions by developing the skills for organizing, regulating and situating behavior in accordance with the demands of school settings and situations

Principles of Teaching Self-Discipline Skills

Self-discipline instruction involves teaching students how to take responsibility and ownership for their behavior. As such, it represents something of a change from more teacher-centered notions of discipline and behavior management. Before we turn in subsequent chapters to discussing ways for helping students become more self-reliant in their behavior, we will look more closely at how the concept of self-discipline creates a new focus for addressing the learning and behavior needs of students.

Treating Discipline as a Curricular Concern

Setting self-discipline as one of the instructional aims for your teaching establishes discipline and behavior management as curricular concerns, comparable to the teaching of reading, math, science, social skills and the other instructional content areas. Self-discipline instruction thus follows the same basic principles and framework you follow with teaching in any other curriculum area. Consider for a moment that throughout their schooling typical students learn to manage their behavior in a variety of ways. They learn such things as:

— setting goals and priorities for their behavior,

— pacing themselves in completing tasks and activities,

— applying themselves to their work,

— directing their behavior along acceptable channels of performance,

— making judgments and decisions about their actions,

— moderating their actions in accordance with the expectations of teachers and peers.

These aspects of learning are part of the central core of what students learn in school. But many approaches to discipline and management overlook this and focus on teacher-directed ways of controlling behavior rather than on promoting student self-reliance. If instead we view discipline as a curricular issue, it becomes clear that our real task is teaching students to take responsibility for their actions.

Focusing on Desired Rather Than Problem Behavior

An instructional approach to self-discipline, like any good pedagogy, begins by analyzing the desired performance and setting goals for students to attain. The key to planning self-discipline instruction is developing a full understanding of the competent performance you wish your students to learn. This is because promoting responsibility, ownership and self-discipline is defined by the things you want students to do, not by the misbehavior you want them to avoid. Therefore, as you consider the concept of self-discipline and the ways it affects student behavior, you will shift your focus from the problems of students who lack self-discipline to the kinds of behavior that constitute successful,

> "Because self-discipline is learned more or less incidentally, rather than through deliberate curricular instruction, we often fail to recognize how remarkable and complex it is."

skilled performance. This analysis will help you formulate clear goals and objectives for self-discipline instruction in classroom and other school settings. Furthermore, the information you gain from observing the ways competent students manage their behavior will provide a solid framework for improving the skills of those who display problem behavior. Thus, the approach for students who are at risk or who currently display serious behavior problems is based on the successful performance you want them to learn, rather than on the disruptive or incompetent performance that seems to be the more immediate and pressing concern.

Discipline Becomes a Collaborative Process with the Students

One of the benefits of incorporating self-discipline instruction in your teaching is that it promotes student involvement, even collaboration, in the behavior change process. At the heart of this process is the belief that students have a strong desire to feel autonomous and to have command over factors that affect their everyday lives. With self-discipline instruction, you focus on teaching students to act competently not because they have to, but because they want to. Achieving this level of self-determination requires them to have the skills and the capacity to make informed, thoughtful decisions about how they will behave. In many discipline and management approaches students are merely passive agents, but in teaching self-discipline, their involvement must extend further. The most significant change in their performance occurs when they take responsibility and ownership for their own behavior. Thus, a major focus of self-discipline instruction is on teaching students the skills that enable them to carry out the discipline and management process themselves.

> **"Performance refers to the series of actions students must manage in order to complete a task or activity."**

Dimensions of Self-Discipline

Self-discipline can be thought of as three broad, interrelated dimensions of behavior: **Performance**, **motivation**, and **judgments**. Learning to manage and negotiate each of these areas successfully is crucial to being successful in any school situation or task. The following section introduces each of these elements and gives examples of ways self-discipline skills help students regulate and direct their behavior. The subsequent chapters will explain how you can develop and optimize student ability to manage these dimensions of behavior.

Managing Performance

Performance is the most basic element of self-discipline. This term refers to the series of actions students must manage in order to complete a task or activity. When we speak of the things students do in school — participating in discussions, completing assignments, conversing with classmates and teachers — we are referring not to discrete behavior, but to complex patterns of interlinked actions or steps. Students use self-discipline skills to plan, negotiate and control these steps so they can carry them out correctly. For example, students might need to follow these performance steps when they complete their homework:

— listen to the teacher's explanation of each assignment,

— write assignment directions in their notebooks,

— assemble the necessary books and materials to bring home,

— schedule time at home to do the work,

— complete each of the assignments they were given,

— check their work to make sure they completed all required tasks,

— organize their books and materials to bring back to school,

— check with friends before class about work they completed,

— review assignments with the rest of the class,

— hand in assignments when their teacher requests them.

These elements of performance form the actions students must learn to manage in order to complete their assignments. Performance might also include subtle things like using a particular strategy for answering the questions in an assignment; asking teachers, parents or other students for help when it is needed; and coordinating homework tasks with after school chores or playing with friends.

In order to carry out a series of performance steps like this, students must be able to plan, coordinate and keep track of the required behavior as the activity unfolds. When students fail to manage performance successfully, they usually have difficulty staying on task and completing activities. Certain students, for example, don't complete their homework because they fail to organize or execute their performance correctly; or because they leave out or misplace pivotal steps in the sequence. One student might neglect to write down the assignment properly, another may fail to plan out a routine for doing the work at home, and another may give up rather than asking for help or going on to

> **"Motivation is the driving force for behavior and it comes from the results or outcomes students obtain when they perform a skill or task successfully. Motivation energizes the students' performance by giving them the desire to complete the required actions."**

the next question. Others might leave out performance steps entirely, ignoring the directions you gave, neglecting important parts of an assignment, or forgetting to bring homework to school the next morning. These students may actually have the academic skills and knowledge to get a passing grade on their assignments, but their problems in managing and coordinating the series of performance steps leads them instead to low achievement and frustration.

Managing Motivation

Performance represents the most basic element of a task or activity — the things that students do. But students are not robots; they do not perform these steps automatically or instinctively, but do them for a complex set of reasons. These reasons may involve long-term goals, short-term rewards, or even simple motives like pleasing the teacher or conforming to social norms. Such factors introduce a second dimension of behavior that students must learn to manage, that of **motivation**.

Motivation is the driving force for behavior and it comes from the results or outcomes students obtain when they perform a skill or task successfully. Motivation energizes the students' performance by giving them the desire to complete the required actions. Learning to generate and direct motivation is a key element of self-discipline because it allows students to develop the incentive to carry out the performance steps and to stay on track. The ability to manage motivation helps them sustain concentration and direction in their behavior because they can focus their actions on achieving specific and desired results.

For example, most of your students pay attention to your teaching activities even if they are not inherently interested in what you are saying. They have learned to manage a variety of important outcomes that naturally follow from paying attention. These might include keeping up with the coursework, understanding their assignments, doing better on tests, staying aligned with what the rest of the class is doing, keeping out of trouble with their teacher, and simply feeling satisfied with their own progress and learning. These outcomes come from a variety of sources, both internal and external, and range from obvious to subtle. Making use of these outcomes to derive motivation to stay on task is an important aspect of self-discipline.

On the other hand, you may find at times that your students have trouble harnessing outcomes for paying attention as much as you would like. Their attention may lapse or they may have trouble applying themselves to your instructions because they fail to connect their behavior to the outcomes available. They may not recognize the benefits that result from paying better attention, or they might not value these outcomes, putting more value on the attention they gain from their off-task behavior. Such difficulties may be pronounced in individual students who are at risk of failing. These students are often unable to recognize or value the outcomes that provide motivation for other children, and as a result they pay attention much less than their classmates. For example, some students may be more interested in clowning with their neighbor or looking out the window than in listening to your presentation. Often students like these may not even realize that they are capable of obtaining the rewards that other students achieve, such as earning passing grades or gaining their teacher's respect. As this possibility suggests, students' perception of outcomes is every bit as important as the outcomes themselves. Formulating accurate perceptions of the potential results of performance is an important aspect of learning to manage motivation effectively.

"Judgements. We use the term judgments to designate the decisions about and adjustments in performance students make from cues and feedback in the environment. "

Managing Judgments

By managing performance, students can carry out the actions demanded in a situation. By managing motivation, they can generate the incentive to carry out these actions. But this is not enough to ensure competent performance. While they are performing, students must make constant **judgments** and determinations in order to track their progress and to regulate and adapt their actions to correspond with changes in their circumstances. Students make these kinds of judgments by drawing on information from sources around them. Judgments thus represents a third dimension of behavior students must learn to manage so they can keep their behavior in line with shifting school demands.

We use the term judgments to designate the decisions about and adjustments in performance students make from cues and feedback in the environment. Students might use cues from their surroundings to evaluate how effective their behavior is, to decide what to do next, or to determine when, where, how much, and with whom performance should take place. The information to make these judgments may come from external sources such as classroom structure, teachers and peers, or from internal sources including personal experience, emotions and physical state. These environmental cues give students information about key elements of performance, as well as about their progress toward attaining key outcomes.

Even during a casual activity like conversing with classmates during free time, students need to make important decisions about their behavior: What to say to one another, when to add comments to the discussion, how to react to peer comments, and how to adjust their behavior based on the way their peers respond to their comments and actions. To judge these issues correctly, students monitor many sources of information in the environment, including facial expressions, tone of voice, size of the group, topics being discussed, pauses in conversation, ambient noise from the hallway and the location of their teacher.

When students fail to make these kinds of judgments, their conversations are more likely to end in disputes or hurt feelings. These kinds of problems often arise because the students fail to adequately attend to what others are saying, or they overlook other people's reactions to what they are saying. They may misinterpret the information they obtain by thinking others are insulting them when they are really making a friendly joke or by misreading a neutral facial expression as hostile. Problems may also occur when students do not respond appropriately to the information they receive, such as when they make silly comments or argue when they think they are not being noticed as much as they would like.

Such problems can be particularly notable in at risk students. While most students will have ill-mannered or contentious conversations once in a while, teachers can always point to a few students whose particular lack of skill at making judgments during conversations leads them frequently to act silly or say immature things, to get into loud arguments or even to starting fights with their classmates. Using information to make judgments about performance is thus a key element of self-discipline, and to perform adequately, students must be able to attend to, interpret and react to a variety of cues in the environment around them.

How to Observe Self-Discipline

As a teacher, you naturally focus on the discipline problems your students display because such behavior tends to disrupt the orderly routine of the classroom and makes the students stand out from their peers. But it's also important to understand the skills competent students use to successfully regulate and direct their behavior so you can advance and reinforce these important skills. By acting as a neutral observer and watching the way successful students perform school tasks, you can learn a great deal about their behavior you did not notice before.

Here is a short activity to help you understand some of the ways your students use self-discipline skills, and it shows how the three dimensions of self-discipline are already supported by your favorite teaching methods. The purpose of the activity is twofold. First, it will point out how the three areas of self-discipline might appear in school situations that are familiar to you. Secondly, and more importantly, it will underscore the fact that teaching self-discipline is something that you do every day in the course of your regular teaching practices.

Worksheet 1A shows how Mrs. Wilson completed this activity. As you can see, she has filled out a simple worksheet listing some of her favorite classroom practices in the column on the left, and has noted in the other columns ways that these practices help foster better management of performance, motivation,

> "By acting as a neutral observer and watching the way successful students perform school tasks, you can learn a great deal about their behavior you did not notice before."

and judgments among her students. You can do the same thing using the blank copy of **Worksheet 1A** at the end of the chapter or a worksheet you design yourself. To begin with, list in the first column two or three procedures or methods you think are particularly effective for encouraging self-direction or motivation in your students. These could be activities you use in your own classroom or observed in other school settings. You might list techniques for focusing student attention, systems of rewards or incentives, ways for teaching study habits or subject matter concepts, or procedures for dealing with disruptive behavior.

Once you have listed a few items in the first column, begin considering how these practices help students build better self-discipline in the areas of performance, motivation and judgment. The following suggestions should help you identify a few key points in each area. For performance, look at the ways each procedure helps students plan, organize and sequence the actions they should complete, and the ways it helps them coordinate and integrate their behavior into the flow of classroom activities. For example, Mrs. Wilson noted that teaching her students to use the "five Ws" strategy for thinking about current events topics helps them plan and structure their question-asking more effectively. For motivation, look for ways each practice helps students see the tangible and intangible benefits they receive from performing well, or to link these benefits to specific aspects of performance. Mrs. Wilson wrote that her wall chart showing assignment completion helps students track their daily progress on assignments, highlights successful work completion and sets up friendly competition among students as they compare their grades. Finally, for judgments, list ways each method helps students attend and react to the cues in their environment and make accurate decisions about their behavior. Mrs. Wilson noted that her use of role-playing situations to improve conversational skills helps students rehearse the decisions and judgments they need to make about body language, moods, topics of conversation and other important issues.

As you carry out this activity, you will begin to recognize that teaching self-discipline does not need to involve complicated add-on activities, formalized testing and planning, or advanced degrees of expertise. It is related much more closely to focusing and extending the "best practice" approaches teachers rely on in their classrooms to help students perform in self-directed, coordinated and effective ways. The focus in this book will be on how to organize and harness such practices to improve the self-discipline of groups of students and individuals.

> "Set high standards for your students' behavior and model the actions you want them to display . . . share more of the responsibility for operating the classroom with your students and give them a voice in planning lessons and structuring daily routines . . . tell them how your lessons relate to their academic achievement."

How to Encourage a Climate of Self-Discipline

While the book will focus mostly on teaching self-discipline in a planned, deliberate manner, you can also use many generalized approaches to help your students learn and practice self-discipline skills. One way is to demonstrate these skills in your own teaching behavior. Students normally look up to their teachers and they will often take on the attitudes, moods, and emotions their teachers display. When you set high standards for your students' behavior and model the actions you want them to display, they will often follow your example in their own expectations and interactions. You could also share more of the responsibility for operating the classroom with your students and give them a voice in planning lessons and structuring daily routines. You could tell them how your lessons relate to their academic achievement, discuss when lessons are going well or poorly, and ask them for feedback and suggestions for improving teaching activities. Showing this kind of flexibility in your approach to teaching lessons, to establishing classroom rules, and to structuring procedures and routines will encourage your students to take more ownership for their behavior and for what goes on in the classroom.

"Promote a classroom climate that builds a sense of community and encourages self-discipline."

Another generalized approach is to promote a classroom climate that builds a sense of community that encourages self-discipline. Groups of students usually establish an identity and personality of their own, and they often respond as a unit to the situations and circumstances around them. By cultivating a positive and constructive group personality and channeling it toward your self-discipline aims, you can have an enormous effect on the ways students support and regulate one another's behavior and on the overall approach they take to school and learning. For example, you could work toward building cohesion in the group by structuring tasks and opportunities for students to get to know one another better and encourage working toward common aims. You could stress the benefits of collective use of abilities and talents, and of relying on one another for assistance and support instead of the teacher. You could show them how to make accommodations in their own interactions for differences in abilities and learning styles by highlighting alternative ways of participating in activities. Finally, you could encourage students to oversee and monitor one another's progress, and provide rewards and privileges based on group performance rather than on individual competitiveness. In these ways you could foster an atmosphere of self-discipline in your classroom in which students learn to become more self-directed and -disciplined and to take greater responsibility for their behavior.

Suggestions for Observing, Using Worksheet 1

This worksheet is designed to guide you through a short observation of some of your teaching procedures and you can adapt or augment it to suit your circumstances. Some suggestions for conducting a useful observation are the following:

Keep the observation short

Try observing activities or parts of lessons that are only 10-15 minutes long. Longer observations will diminish your ability to concentrate on the circumstances around you.

Remain unobtrusive while observing

This is particularly important when you observe in a setting where you are not normally present. You should try to arrive early and take a seat in the back or out of the students' line of vision. Try pretending to be busy with reading or correcting papers when the students come in. If it seems like you are not paying attention to them, they are likely to ignore you fairly quickly and you can soon begin observing them more deliberately.

Be aware of your own limitations

If you are observing in your own classroom or setting, keep in mind how difficult it can be to teach and observe at the same time. If you do observe while you are teaching, schedule an activity where you are not actively providing instruction. Pretend you are grading papers or are engaged in some other work while the students are occupied with a specific task or activity.

Consider using outside observers or videotaping

Videotape to gain a more objective view of your own settings. Videotaping an activity can be particularly helpful for later viewing because you can pause the tape to take notes or watch a segment over again to note subtle behaviors.

Watch for student behavior rather than teacher behavior

When observing in another teacher's classroom, avoid being distracted by what she is saying and doing. Remember, your objective is to focus on student actions.

Look for behavior that indicates self-discipline

Rather than focusing on the procedures or routines of the activity, look for ways students direct and regulate their behavior, show restraint in their actions, and maintain their interest and attention in the activities. Also, watch for how students direct the activity their own way toward their own goals. And, observe how they re-focus one another's behavior in task-directed ways through encouragement, redirection and subtle pressure.

With regard to managing performance, note such factors as:

— The ways they break a complicated task into more manageable steps,

— The ways they carry out directions in ways that fit their own learning and performance strategies,

— The ways they share information about tasks and expectations,

— The ways they vary the pace or speed of their actions to fit task demands,

— The ways they negotiate differences of opinion and express their views,

With regard to managing motivation, look for:

— The ways they motivate themselves by making a game of an activity, by self-competitiveness or by setting other self-created outcomes,

— The ways they offer subtle support and encouragement to one another,

— The ways they re-focus when they have become distracted or off-task.

With regard to managing judgments, watch for:

— The ways they seek out feedback to ensure they are on the right track,

— The ways they determine whether or not they are keeping up with the group,

— The ways they judge whether they are on the right track or need to correct mistakes.

Don't try to do too much

The idea is to begin developing a general notion of how students manage performance, motivation and judgments. You need not be exhaustive in your list, nor develop a full understanding of the skills students use in these activities. Instead, think of this as practicing a new way to look at student behavior.

Worksheet 1 Example

Ms. Wilson teaches in a special education resource room at Lincoln Middle School. Some general education teachers have been coming to her with reports about discipline problems students on her case load are having and asking for suggestions to improve their behavior. Mr. Thompson, the English teacher, said one of the students is acting out in his class and a couple others seem unmotivated and inattentive, get off track in group work and rarely get their papers in on time. Mrs. Lacey, the science teacher, expressed similar concerns about the lack of initiative, organization and motivation some of the students are showing. Ms. Wilson rarely has an opportunity to work with the students outside the resource room setting. Although she is used to the ways they behave during small-group and one-on-one activities, where they normally do well under her close direction, she doesn't feel she has a good basis for suggesting procedures that might work in a large group setting.

She met with Mrs. Parsons, who has three of the students in her 7th grade social studies class. Mrs. Parsons said she had to work with the students initially to get them involved with classmates, but since then she has been impressed with how well they have been participating in activities and progressing in the material. She explained that she encourages self-discipline from the beginning of the year and structures lessons and activities so that students learn to organize and mange their own behavior. She noted that most students, especially those who are at risk or in special education, seem to be fitting in well and benefiting from this approach.

Ms. Wilson looked over some of Mrs. Parson's lesson plans, but she feels that she would learn a lot more about Mrs. Parson's approach by watching the students while class was going on. Mrs. Parsons agreed that this would be a worthwhile experience, so Ms. Wilson set aside time to observe a couple of short activities. While she was observing in the classroom, she took some notes on a blank sheet of paper, paying particular attention when students directed and regulated their own behavior, rather than following specific teacher instruction, which she didn't think was a major problem for them. When she was finished, she talked with Mrs. Parsons about her approach to classroom management and discipline, the different behaviors students showed, and improvements they were making in their performance, motivation and judgments, areas Mrs. Parsons has been concentrating on during the year. Together they looked over Ms. Wilson's notes on the worksheet shown in **Worksheet 1**. This format allowed Ms. Wilson to begin to see how the students were learning to take responsibility for important aspects of behavior and developing skills for becoming more self-reliant and successful in school. She told Mrs. Parsons she had never considered how many different kinds of skills are needed by students in these types of activities. She said this information will be helpful to her in her own classroom and in working with other teachers.

Worksheet 1: Observing the dimensions of self-discipline

Name: _Ms. Wilson_ Date: _September 12_

Grade level/student group observed: _Mrs. Parson's 7th grade social studies_

TASK/ACTIVITY OBSERVED	WAYS TASK/ACTIVITY PROMOTES MANAGING:		
	PERFORMANCE	**MOTIVATION**	**JUDGEMENTS**
Using 5 W's question asking strategy in current events discussions	Students plan out questions ahead of time and are coming up with a lot of their own questions without teacher direction	Students are asking good questions — their questions are on-task and get attention and encouragement from Mrs. Parson's and fellow students	Students catch themselves before asking questions to make sure they are in the W's format
	Students are talking about events broadly — extending beyond the textbook material		
Posting daily assignment grades on our wall chart	Students pay close attention to the directions and review directions before turning in work	Students compare their daily scores — some encourage friends to try to do better	Students check answers they're not sure of before turning in the work
	Students check their assignment books to make sure they have directions written correctly.	Students see a connection between taking their time with answers and getting good scores	Students correct wrong answers themselves and ask Mrs. Parson to change grades
Using role playing of historical events to build better conversational skills	Students plan out their dialogues so they stay on specific topics — they work out the steps of the dialogues ahead of time	Students comment on the benefits of preparing and practicing dialogues ahead of time — "That went better this time."	Students are choosing their roles based on context cues — historical background, mood/tone of speaker
	In their dialogues students wait for the speaker to finish before responding so the narration flows well	Students give each other encouraging nods and smiles when the role play goes well. They also look to the audience for applause and recognition.	Students use body language to judge their role play responses - e.g. "President Roosevelt looks like he's getting angry so I should . . ."
			Students judge from the audience's response whether they are "hamming it up" too much or staying in character.

Worksheet 1: Observing the dimensions of self-discipline

Name: _____ Date: _____

Grade level/student group observed: _____

TASK/ACTIVITY OBSERVED	WAYS TASK/ACTIVITY PROMOTES MANAGING:		
	PERFORMANCE	MOTIVATION	JUDGEMENTS

Turning Problems of Discipline into Self-Discipline Goals

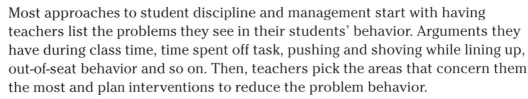

Addressing Problem Behavior —
With Self-Discipline Instruction

Most approaches to student discipline and management start with having teachers list the problems they see in their students' behavior. Arguments they have during class time, time spent off task, pushing and shoving while lining up, out-of-seat behavior and so on. Then, teachers pick the areas that concern them the most and plan interventions to reduce the problem behavior.

While addressing behaviors in this manner may help with your immediate concerns, it doesn't get to the heart of the matter. Most discipline problems are actually manifestations of deficits in self-discipline: Difficulties in managing performance, in managing motivation and in managing judgments. Students who haven't learned the performance steps for handling disagreements will often start arguing; students who haven't learned to be motivated from paying attention in class will often get off-task; and students who haven't learned to judge their social interactions will often push and shove. Disciplinary measures directed toward reducing problem behavior may give you short-term, stopgap ways for getting through the school day, but they do little to teach students needed self-discipline skills.

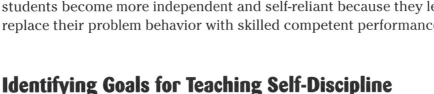
"A focus on teaching self-discipline is more far reaching and beneficial than a problem-centered approach because it concentrates on giving students the skills to manage and regulate their own behavior."

A focus on teaching self-discipline is more far reaching and beneficial than a problem-centered approach because it concentrates on giving students the skills to manage and regulate their own behavior. Learning these skills helps them overcome deficits in their behavior and teaches competent ways of acting in situations that previously caused them difficulties. When students learn the skills for handling disagreements, they have less of a need to argue and build stronger peer relationships. When students learn skills for generating motivation from the outcomes of paying attention, they develop solid, functional reasons for staying on task. By teaching self-discipline, you help students become more independent and self-reliant because they learn how to replace their problem behavior with skilled competent performance.

Identifying Goals for Teaching Self-Discipline

The place to begin teaching self-discipline, as with any instructional area, is in choosing goals you want students to achieve and determining the skills they need to reach them. Chapter 1 discussed how self-discipline is involved in every aspect of school performance, academic and non-academic, so you have a wide range of goals to choose from. Here we give some guidelines for weighing these options so you select the one or two most important goals for your students.

Goals for Teaching Self-Discipline to Groups

Teachers naturally think of discipline after problems arise, but one real advantage of teaching self-discipline to groups is that you can take a proactive role in promoting competent behavior by addressing areas of concern before difficulties become prominent. You can give students opportunities to build and practice important skills and to take a stronger role in promoting a positive and productive environment for learning. Teaching self-discipline to groups also provides a framework for addressing individual problems in behavior when they do arise.

Most teachers will select self-discipline goals that are appropriate for their entire classroom of students, but on some occasions you may wish to choose goals for a specific sub-group. For instance, you might focus on a small group of students who share similar skill needs, such as those who need to improve their homework. You could target class leaders, or decide to work with the whole class, while concentrating in small groups on more individualized concerns.

The goals you select for the group can pertain to almost any area: Specific reading or math activities you wish to concentrate on, study habits you would like students to use more proficiently, areas of class participation that would engage them more in lessons, social and play skills for use on the playground or any number of other goals. **Worksheet 2** shows a form Mrs. Langley used to list goals she is considering for her fifth grade class. You might wish to use a similar format yourself. A blank copy of the worksheet is at the end of the chapter.

On her worksheet Mrs. Langley entered potential goals in four areas: Academic achievement, participation in classroom or school activities, social behavior and physical and emotional development. She used the format "Learn to . . ." to express her goals because it will help her direct her teaching on the major instructional issues she hopes to address for the students. You might wish to use a similar format with your students and add to the list, or you can adapt it to suit your needs. As the examples in Worksheet 2 suggest, your goals should focus broadly on the important aims at the heart of student learning, development and success in school.

> **"Take a proactive role in promoting competent behavior by addressing areas of concern before difficulties become prominent."**

Goals for Teaching Self-Discipline to Individuals

While group instruction is often the best approach for improving skill development with several students at once, sometimes a student will need more personalized attention. Individuals whose self-discipline is less developed than those of their classmates, or who show significant and longstanding behavior problems benefit from well-planned and clearly-targeted instruction. It is usually easy to identify students who have significant problems in self-discipline because their behaviors make them stand out from their peers. When you consider which students to work with, look for those whose performance consistently falls below the level of their classmates.

Elements to watch for include:

— Students whose problems are longstanding and pervasive,

— Students whose problems are multidimensional and complex,

— Students whose difficulties have been resistant to more straightforward attempts at correction,

— Students who show problems in more than one class or with more than one teacher,

— Students whose problems affect their overall performance at school.

Remember to consider not only students whose behavior is extroverted, loud or aggressive, but also students whose problems make them isolated, sullen or withdrawn. Such behavior is often ignored by teachers because it does not disrupt the class, but it can have just as destructive an effect on student productivity and happiness as the more conspicuous behavior of others.

Once you have identified an individual to work with, you may find it helpful to prepare a short description of his behavior, including deficits and strengths. Whether you write a few paragraphs, or simply list behaviors, this task will help to identify key issues you want to address. Moreover, it will give you a checkpoint to refer back to as planning progresses, and will help ensure that you keep your focus on student strengths as well as weaknesses.

As you consider problems or deficits in student behavior, you define goals to address these difficulties. These goals should describe typical, competent behaviors the student would use to replace the inept or disruptive ones currently shown. These types of goals will focus instruction on individual student difficulties without creating special or unusual standards and requirements for them, because they are based on behaviors all students must master. For example, a goal for a student who is frequently off-task might be "Learn to participate actively in class discussions." This goal represents the competent performance the teacher expects of all her students, and directly addresses several problem behaviors the student may display, such as getting out of the seat, distracting neighbors and making outlandish comments. Appendix A provides several examples of goals matched to various problem areas such as noncompliance, aggression and impulsive behavior.

"Consider not only students whose behavior is extroverted, loud or aggressive, but also students whose problems make them isolated, sullen or withdrawn."

The goals you choose for teaching self-discipline to students receiving special education can easily be incorporated into the planning of individualized instructional or management programs. Your self-discipline goals will compliment or enhance academic achievement goals, social goals, vocational goals, and other goals you are entering on student Individual Education Plans (IEPs), Functional Behavior Plans and Individual Transition Plans (ITPs).

By matching individual goals with those you have for typical students, your instruction brings student behavior into line with that of classmates. Thus, self-discipline goals for individuals should be based not on your ideals, but on the same school goals all students are expected to achieve.

Choosing a Single Goal for Instruction

Instruction is most effective when it's directed toward teaching one area of behavior at a time. Teaching often fails to achieve results when teachers try to address too many problems at once or when they set goals beyond students' reach. Establishing goal priorities is an important factor in ensuring success because it gives a clear, sharp and realistic focus to your planning.

When you choose a single goal to work on, your first inclination might be to concentrate on problems that are the most obvious or irritating to you. You may think of students' uncooperative behavior or their tendency to argue in class because these problems are most noticeable and disruptive. But it's important to consider whether there are other more pressing self-discipline needs. Your intent in selecting a goal should be to direct your efforts on the particular area that can produce the most profound improvement in student behavior.

The process of selecting a single goal for teaching self-discipline is simpler than it seems. List the various goals you are considering on a worksheet like the one in **Worksheet 2**, and decide which is the highest priority for instruction.

"Establishing goal priorities is the most important factor in ensuring the success of your instruction because it gives a clear, sharp, and realistic focus to your planning."

Goals for teaching to groups should be ones:

— where many students have difficulties,

— that promote unity and collaboration in the group,

— that improve overall achievement and performance,

— that students enjoy learning,

— that provide a foundation for further development and progress.

Goals for teaching to individuals should be ones:

— that replace or diminish problem behavior,

— that promote more involvement in class or school activities,

— that are highly functional or involves behavior that would be frequently used by the student,

— where improvements in behavior are likely to carry over to other settings and situations,

— that increase the student's status or self-esteem,

— that provide the framework for teaching more advanced self-discipline skills.

You can see in **Worksheet 1** that Mrs. Langley assigned priority levels to the goals on her list and entered them next to each item. Priority 1 items are the one or two goals she would like to address right away, Priority 2 she would like to get to in the next few weeks or months, while Priority 3 can wait longer or be passed on to next year's teacher. Note that these decisions do not mean that Mrs. Langley will neglect to promote other goals as she usually would; the priority numbers designate areas she is most interested in addressing with extra lessons and other activities.

The worksheet indicates that Mrs. Langley has assigned the highest priority to, "Learn to cooperate with other students." She feels that enhancing students' ability to work together will provide a good framework for improving self-discipline skills. She plans to focus on teaching them how to take more responsibility for helping one another with assigned tasks, to plan tasks and activities as a small group, to be more task-oriented and respectful in their interactions with one another and to use other important cooperative skills.

Choosing an Activity or Task as the Context for Instruction

Choosing instructional goals to work on is the most essential element for your teaching. Next, decide on circumstances in which to direct your planning. Teaching self-discipline should usually take place in the context of a particular task or activity that is a regular part of the school routine for students. This approach has two benefits. First, it limits the scope of instruction and gives lessons focus as students acquire and practice new skills. Second, it promotes an emphasis on a discrete set of skills that students can use immediately in everyday situations.

For example, if Mrs. Langley tried to teach her students how to cooperate with one another, the lessons will not be as effective as when she teaches them how to cooperate during small group discussions, at independent work times or during games on the playground. Furthermore, by identifying in advance the exact circumstances she wants students to work on, she makes it clear which self-discipline skills she is teaching. Mrs. Langley decided to direct her teaching on small group discussion activities in her first period English class. She then carries over her instruction to other settings and situations if needed after students have learned self-discipline skills that help them be successful in this setting.

Choosing a single student or group to work with and picking an activity or task to focus on allows you to begin planning lessons with an understanding of the context in which teaching takes place. These decisions, in turn, help narrow your efforts and concentrate them on skill areas that benefit students the most.

Special Ed in a General Ed Setting

Special education teachers should base teaching goals on the needs students have in general education settings, rather than in a separate environment. This guideline will help you direct instruction on skills students can use in the general education environment, even if you must make adaptations in teaching these skills. If you aren't familiar with general education settings, talk with the teachers about their goals and the tasks and activities their students engage in, or observe them directly yourself. Then when you plan instruction, you will be able to tailor your procedures to the specific demands of these activities.

Who Has Time to Teach Self-Discipline?

This question reflects a common feeling among teachers not used to thinking of self-discipline as a regular part of their teaching responsibilities. Special educators and others who work in collaborative teaching situations may have difficulty convincing colleagues to set aside class time for the planning involved in teaching these skills. But when you consider the interrupted class time and lost teaching opportunities caused by student problem behavior, it's clear that teaching self-discipline makes class time more productive and useful. Remember, that self-discipline is a fundamental element in all student achievement and success in school, and teaching these skills fits in naturally with every classroom and school routine. Teachers unwilling to devote instructional time to self-discipline skills overlook the role they play in everyday classroom activities.

N.C. WESLEYAN COLLEGE
ELIZABETH BRASWELL PEARSALL LIBRARY

Suggestions for Using Worksheet 2

Worksheet 2 will help you set a single goal for teaching self-discipline. Use it to list potential goals for students, set goal priorities and describe the context for your teaching plans. The following are suggestions for using the worksheet:

Describe specific and concrete goals

These types of goals help you direct your teaching on observable and teachable behavior rather than attitudes, dispositions or other non-teachable attributes. "Learn to wait turn when speaking" is a better goal than "Learn to control impulses."

Describe goals in positive terms

The goals you list should help to concentrate teaching on competent replacement behavior rather than on reducing or eliminating problem behavior. "Learn to read and follow directions" is better than "Learn to stop wasting class time."

Consider a wide range of goals

Be careful not to limit your list to teacher-set rules and other areas that make for a mostly teacher-directed or teacher-centered environment. Include goals with broader, longer term benefits to students and goals the students themselves would like to achieve.

Set a teaching focus that's helpful to students

Because instructional time is limited, concentrate your efforts on highest priority goals. Your aim in setting a teaching focus should be to make students successful and more productive in school, not to address particular areas that bother you the most.

Look for goals that are educationally sound targets for students

Even if your students are in a separate or self-contained environment, keep your focus on skills needed in general education settings. Teaching students how to perform during activities that take place only in special education classrooms or resource rooms may limit the skill acquisitions that are more applicable to general education classrooms and other inclusive environments.

Give highest priority to one or two items

The worksheet is designed to help you quickly consider many possible goals for instruction, and then settle on a single goal to begin planning. If you identify several Priority 1 items, you still have to decide which will be the primary focus of instructional planning. Remember, you can always go back to the list when you have begun the lessons and plan for a Priority 2 item you had put off.

Avoid choosing tasks or activities that occur occasionally

The context for your teaching should be a frequent and integral part of student daily routine to give you plenty of opportunities to teach and reinforce needed skills. Occasional activities, like giving a semester project report or going for a weekly library visit, don't provide enough opportunities for learning and applying self-discipline skills on a regular basis.

Worksheet 2 Example

Mrs. Langley is a fifth grade teacher at Harrison Elementary School. This year's class is one of the most challenging since she started teaching. From the start of the year, she has been dealing with student misbehavior and it's getting worse each week. Now, a few students don't seem able to control themselves or even care about her rules and disciplinary measures. "If I get in trouble, so what?" is their attitude. Mrs. Langley feels she has to be constantly on them for their behavior. If she isn't, they get out of their seats; whisper to each other while she is talking; interrupt when other students are answering; criticize, argue, and make fun of each other; don't get their work done and more. She tells other teachers: "If my students would work as hard on their school work as they do at impressing their friends or causing trouble, they would be excellent students. I know my class could do better if they would only put their minds to it."

After some soul searching and retrenchment, Mrs. Langley concludes that her attempts to discipline the class are not working; rather it's causing the room atmosphere to be more negative and combative each day. She knows she has to take a more direct and positive approach and teach them how to become more self-disciplined. She decides to concentrate on her first period English class that sets the tone for the rest of the day. She starts by listing a wide range of goals for the group to accomplish to get a sense of where they're at and what they need to work on. She then sets goal priorities to give more focus to her planning. She considers how each goal affects the overall personality of the group and the quality of their work habits and interactions. She assigns, "Learn to cooperate with other students," as her number 1 priority. She feels that focusing the group on working towards common, positive aims will give students an opportunity to interact in a civil and productive manner. This goal also gives her a framework for teaching them about taking responsibility for regulating and directing behaviors toward achieving other positive ends as well, like getting assignments completed on time and showing patience and respect toward one another. To narrow her planning further, Mrs. Langley chooses "small group discussion" as the context for her first lessons. She feels that with this activity, she can target a discrete set of skills students can use everyday in realistic classroom situations. Later she can branch out from this activity and the English class to other parts of the school day.

Worksheet 2: Setting priorities for teaching self-discipline.

Name: ___Mrs. Langley_____ Date: _September 20_

Student or group: ___English class_____ Grade: _5____

Goals for Teaching:	Priority Level (1, 2, or 3):
Goals related to academic achievement	
Learn to complete homework, projects, tests and other assignments	2
Learn to understand the concepts presented in the English curriculum	2
Learn to use work and study habits needed for learning the material	2
Goals related to participation in classroom or school activities	
Learn to ask questions when help is needed	2
Learn to follow the rules and routines of the setting or activity	3
Learn to comply with teacher directions for assignments and activities	2
Learn to follow along and complete tasks and activities	3
Learn to pay attention in class and participate actively	2
Goals related social behavior	
Learn to make friends and get along with classmates	3
Learn to cooperate with teachers and classmates	1
Learn to play games and participate in recreational activities	3
Learn to respect others and their belongings	3
Learn to show sensitivity for the moods and feelings of others	1
Goals related to physical and emotional development	
Learn to maintain good health and hygiene, e.g., wear coats in cold weather, wash hands after using the bathroom	3
Learn to use class and personal time productively	3
Learn to take responsibility and initiative for learning and achievement	2
Learn to take initiative in dealing with own problems	3

Worksheet 2: Setting priorities for teaching self-discipline.

Name: _____ Date: _____

Student or group: _____ Grade: _____

Goals for Teaching:	Priority Level (1, 2, or 3):
Goals related to academic achievement	
Goals related to participation in classroom or school activities	
Goals related social behavior	
Goals related to physical and emotional development	

Chapter 3

Managing Performance

Self-Discipline and Performance

Chapter 1 discussed how performance requires carrying out a sequence of inter-connected steps in completing a task or activity, and how competent performance is the progression through this sequence with a minimum of forethought and deliberation. Consider for a moment how your own students would go through the steps outlined in Chapter 1 for doing a homework assignment or having a conversation with friends in the cafeteria. Successful and competent students display these behaviors in an orderly fashion without hesitation. It's self-discipline skills that make this process easy for students and help them organize and coordinate performance steps to complete tasks and activities in an orderly and efficient manner.

By comparison, students who do poorly at managing their performance experience delays, confusion, frustration or failure because they leave out important steps, place them out of sequence or carry them out incorrectly or inefficiently. You can sometimes help these students overcome their difficulties by using basic instructional techniques, such as by making directions more explicit, having the students imitate classmates' behavior, or showing them better ways for doing tasks. Such methods can counteract problems in managing performance, as students' increased attention and practice help them learn to carry out actions more effectively. But when performance required by a task is complicated, or when problems students have are challenging, consider observing student behavior and investigating their needs before beginning instruction.

Observing Student Performance to Determine Instructional Needs

In this section we will discuss an approach for analyzing the performance required to achieve your self-discipline goals and assessing the difficulties students might have in managing this performance. Whether you are planning instruction for a group of students or an individual, it's helpful to conduct observations of the tasks or activities related to your goals. This allows you to look carefully at how students execute each step in the sequence and identify steps they must learn to manage more effectively. You can do this in three-stages:

Stage 1: Identify essential steps of the task or activity,

Stage 2: Plan the best way to observe these steps,

Stage 3: Conduct observations and note the steps that need the most attention.

Worksheet 3 at the end of the chapter shows how Mr. Elsworth used this approach to conduct observations in his ninth grade class. A blank copy of the worksheet is provided to aid your planning.

The first stage helps you determine specific demands of a task or activity before doing the observation. This information will focus your observation on the positive behaviors students need to work on, rather than on problem behaviors you see. Start by considering the beginning and ending steps students perform in successfully completing the activity. Beginning steps may be watching for teacher directions, moving to a new area, greeting teachers or peers, or getting out materials. Ending steps may be turning in assignments, making closing remarks, cleaning up materials or moving to another task.

After identifying the first and last steps, list in chronological order essential steps students need to follow. For example, Ms. Jacobs, a second grade teacher, might describe the following steps a successful student performs in a typical reading activity:

— sits down and pulls chair close to other group members,

— talks with neighbors excitedly,

— quiets down when teacher directs,

— finds story in book,

— volunteers for teacher questions,

— shows excitement about wanting to read next (sits up, waves hand in air, etc.),

— reads carefully,

— looks for approval from teacher when finished reading,

— follows along in book when others are reading,

— offers help and encouragement to peers (pointing out place, whispering difficult words),

— shows curiosity about story,

— relates story to personal experiences during discussion,

— closes book, gathers materials and begins talking to neighbors when activity ends,

— helps put chairs back before returning to desk.

Worksheet 3 shows the list of steps for "working on assignments in small groups" that Mr. Elsworth prepared for his students. As these examples show, the list you make need not be exhaustive, but it should describe the demands for the task or activity. You are then able to use the list to observe the elements

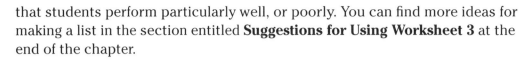

that students perform particularly well, or poorly. You can find more ideas for making a list in the section entitled **Suggestions for Using Worksheet 3** at the end of the chapter.

In Stage Two, planning your observation, the question you need to address is, "What will be the best way or ways to observe the steps I have listed?" Most often you can watch students do the activity. This is most effective when the task or activity doesn't require a lot of active input from the teacher. When you are too actively engaged in teaching to closely observe performance, you may wish to videotape the activity and watch it later or have a colleague help you observe. Here, the list you prepared in the first stage can be a valuable tool for explaining to your colleague what they should look for.

Conduct at least three to five observations of student behavior and carry them out unobtrusively. The observations should be short enough in duration to not make unreasonable demands on your (or the observer's) attention. You may wish to look at the beginning of the activity one day, the middle of it the next, and so on. The idea is to determine the best way to gain an accurate appraisal of how well your students perform the key steps that comprise your list.

The third stage is the simplest, once you have completed planning. The main guideline when conducting observations is to keep an open mind. By using the list of steps to help guide your observations, look at how students respond to a full range of demands during the activity. As you observe, the list can serve as a helpful checklist for recording your observations. Focus on the behaviors and issues that are your biggest concerns, but be open to surprises or new discoveries. You will often find that student performance of certain steps is a lot better or more consistent than you thought. On the other hand, you may find that they have a lot of difficulty with steps you had not considered a problem before. You can make notes next to the list indicating which steps represent strengths and weaknesses. For example, Mr. Elsworth used +'s to represent the skilled performance of his students and 0's to designate unskilled performance. This evaluative approach can be particularly useful for outside observers as it makes it very clear what you wish them to look for. At the same time, you or another observer should note any unusual occurrences, general trends, or behavior issues you might have overlooked before. This kind of spur-of-the-moment insight can often be useful for guiding instructional planning.

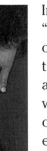

"Unfortunately, teachers usually notice problem behavior when it becomes excessive or disruptive, so it's easy to miss the root cause of a student's difficulties, and it is just as easy to overlook the things the student does do well."

Observing Individual Students

Investigating the needs of individual students is even more crucial than observing behavior of groups. Too often, teachers plan instruction based on preconceptions about a student's problems without taking an objective look at the student's behavior. Unfortunately, teachers usually notice problem behavior when it becomes excessive or disruptive, so it's easy to miss the root cause of a student's difficulties, and it is just as easy to overlook the things the student does do well. Conducting a few observations will help you consider the full range of student behavior, and identify the best places to address problem areas before they become more disruptive.

An important principle in observing individual students is not comparing their behavior to the idealized behavior we would like them to display, but rather to the actual, average or "C-level" behavior displayed by their peers. Then, when carrying out observations, focus on the average, basic skills students need to learn rather than on the negative behaviors they display or the ideal performance you think they should be showing. Your results will then aid in planning realistic and attainable objectives for the students.

What do I Watch for When Observing Performance?

As you carry out observations, step out of your role as teacher and view student behavior from their own perspective. This helps you determine more accurately the types of difficulties they have managing their performance. The following are things to look for during your observations to decide how successfully the students manage individual steps and the overall sequence:

— Are students prepared to start the activity, e.g., are they seated properly, do they have their materials, are they ready to listen to directions?

— Do they start with the first step, or do they start at the wrong point?

— Do they perform individual steps successfully, or do they have difficulty with some of them? Are some steps too confusing, complex or daunting for them and cause a breakdown in the sequence? Do they simply forget to do some of them?

— Do they perform the steps in a proper sequence? Is there a deliberate ordering to their behavior, or are their actions random or directionless?

— Do they perform all the steps or skip some of them? Do they organize their behavior with a set goal in mind, or are they just going through the motions?

— Do they coordinate their performance with other people's behavior? Do they follow the basic rules and routines for the situation, like seeking help from classmates at the proper times and in the proper manner?

— Do they make adjustments in the steps or in the sequence to fit ongoing circumstances? Do they respond to changes in conditions and make any necessary shifts?

— Do they adapt the steps to fit their own characteristics, preferences and learning styles? Do they look for alternative ways of doing things that might be easier or more effective for them?

— Do they end with the last step in the sequence? Do they know when they have finished meeting the demands of the situation?

Your observations may also point to difficulties managing motivation or judgments, and Chapters 4 and 5 will address these areas in detail. Managing performance is the most basic element of self-discipline and your planning in this area will provide a solid framework for teaching regardless of the dimension you emphasize in your lessons.

Defining Instructional Objectives

Once you understand the steps that cause problems for students and some of the reasons for them, set instructional objectives that address the most significant areas affecting their performance. These objectives should focus on the three to five aspects of behavior you wish to teach students to manage more effectively. They may represent individual performance steps, groups of related steps, or over arching skills that apply to all the steps in the sequence.

On his worksheet Mr. Elsworth listed these objectives:

1. learn to listen to or read directions before starting work,

2. learn to handle disagreements without arguing,

3. learn to ask neighbors for help and to give them help,

4. learn to coordinate work with others in the group.

He defined the first three objectives because in his observations he noticed students were inconsistent in carrying out these steps, and he thinks it's crucial for their success in cooperative work. He added the fourth objective to express his general concern about the difficulties students have working together.

Lesson plans must be grounded in a clear understanding of behavior areas you want students to manage more effectively. Establish a sharp focus for your teaching by analyzing performance steps, observing student behavior and setting instructional objectives. The last section of the chapter discusses procedures for teaching students the skills for managing performance.

Teaching Skills for Managing Performance

There are three types of self-discipline skills that help students manage their performance successfully: **Organizing**, **coordinating** and **personalizing** performance.

1. Organizing Performance

The most fundamental aspect of self-discipline is the ability to identify which elements of behavior to include in performance, and to order these into a sequence of steps that meet behavioral demands. This means being able to tell what to do and when to do it. While that sounds simple, it can involve complex skills.

Organizing performance includes:

— understanding what needs to be accomplished by a task or activity under the circumstances for performance,

— deciding on the elements that are involved in completing the task or activity,

— breaking down or "chunking" elements into a series of manageable steps or sub-tasks so the individual actions are not too complex or daunting,

— anticipating upcoming steps and preparing for them ahead of time when necessary,

— sequencing behavior to begin and end with the proper steps, and to include all the appropriate intervening steps,

— grouping related steps so they flow together smoothly,

— executing the steps to fit the time available,

— integrating the performance of single steps with the performance of other steps in the sequence to form a fluent and well-timed behavior pattern,

— scheduling specific times to carry out the performance steps, e.g., during class, study hall, or evening hours.

In order to do an assignment, students have to know the steps they need to complete, from listening to the teacher's directions to turning in the completed work. They would also have to know how to order the steps in a sequential fashion and group those that naturally go together. They have to listen to the directions and ask questions before getting out their materials and beginning the work. They might group these steps together, but they would have to wait with the others until they are confident they understand the directions. The students would also have to link what they do during prior steps to what they do in the later steps. Early on, they need to anticipate possible difficulties by asking the teacher to clarify the assignment. Later, when they are working during study time or at home, they may have to call a classmate or look to a parent for help on more specific problems. In this way they can carry out the sequence of steps in a fluent and efficient manner. Of course, much of this organizing is done implicitly and without a lot of conscious thought. When students ask questions before starting on an assignment, they do not think of this as breaking their performance into sequential steps, but that's what they're doing. Thus, organizing performance helps students plan and sequence their behavior to correspond to the demands of the situation.

Teaching Students to Organize Performance

One way to help students learn to organize their behavior is to show them how to follow a list of performance steps for a specific task or activity. An outline, checklist or mental inventory of steps can give students an overview of the task they need to perform and indicate precisely what they need to accomplish. In their simplest form, these lists serve as prompts or reminders to draw attention to the most important steps. In more detailed form, they help students relate individual steps to the overall performance sequence, giving them a precise explanation of actions they should carry out and the way they link together.

Other ways to use lists to organize student performance:

— develop step-by-step picture displays for how to put away toys or do a project at an activity center,

— prepare an outline of the steps for doing a science experiment or book report,

— present samples of completed art or crafts projects that highlight key elements in completing the steps,

— develop notebook sheets, logs or personal planners for writing out the steps for homework assignments,

— assign computer exercises that review the steps for doing math problems,

— show film strips, or provide audio- or videotapes or other media that show the steps for sports activities or industrial arts projects.

Such approaches work best when you involve students in the planning and execution of the procedures. They might assist in planning the list of steps, describe them in their own words, or demonstrate how to follow them in a role-playing activity. Procedures like these include students in the teaching and stimulate greater self-discipline and independence.

Another way of promoting organization is to teach students how to structure their own behavior in ways that accomplish tasks. They could learn how to break them down into steps or sub-tasks that are manageable and doable for them in much the same way that you would prepare a list of steps. The process is fairly simple and involves showing students how to:

— describe the task that needs to be completed,

— identify a clear beginning point for the task,

— identify a clear ending point for the task,

— specify intervening steps or actions,

— sequence the steps in a way that accomplishes the objective.

Steps students plan don't have to be exactly the same as those in your analysis, as long as they fulfill the essential demands of the goal you are teaching.

Sometimes it's easier for students to organize steps by memorizing one formalized sequence applied across a number of situations. Mnemonic devices and behavior strategies are two systematic ways of helping students memorize performance steps. Examples you might find familiar are:

— "Thirty days hath September . . ." to remember the number of days in each month.

— "My very elegant mother just served us nine pizzas" to remember the order of the planets.

Mnemonic devices serve as cues for behavior and they have the added benefit of being self-regulated, because students can use them to prompt their own behavior rather than relying on cues from the teacher.

Behavior strategies are formal routines that give students a single, consistent way of carrying out the steps in a task or activity. They help students develop a mental habit that unifies their behavior. Once students learn how to follow the strategy, the strategy itself, and the words or letters that represent the strategy, serve as prompts in how to do each of the major steps in an activity. Some examples of strategies are:

— **RAP** (for understanding written material) – **R**ead (a paragraph, section, etc.), **A**sk yourself "What were the main ideas?", **P**ut the ideas in your own words

— **SQ3R** (for writing reports and responding to questions) – **S**urvey the material looking for headings and major points, **Q**uestion what is to be learned in each section, **R**ead the answer, **R**ecite or write notes about the major points covered in the section, and **R**eview the notes and see if they are accurate.

— **6-W** approach to writing (for writing reports) – have students follow an outline of "**w**ho," "**w**hat," "**w**here," "**w**hen," "**w**hy" and "ho**w**" questions.

You don't need to rely on pre-developed strategies; you or your students can invent your own techniques for the particular areas you want to work on.

2. Coordinating Performance

In addition to being organized, performance must also be well-timed and placed to fit with the environment and the activities in the setting. **Coordinating** performance involves correlating and integrating individual steps with other things that are going on. Coordinating performance involves:

— modifying and adapting behavior to changes in environmental conditions,

— aligning performance with the behavior of other people, and with ongoing events and activities,

— continuing the performance sequence after it has been interrupted by other activities,

— integrating performance with other responsibilities, tasks or activities that may be required at the same time,

— drawing on people and resources that can assist with completing steps effectively, e.g., classmates, library materials, study aids.

Coordinating performance is especially important when students need to integrate their behavior with the actions of other people or align their actions with circumstances that are changeable, like taking part in small group activities, having conversations with friends or playing games during recess. When participating in class discussions, for example, students must coordinate comments they would like to make with what their classmates and teachers are saying. They must recognize which comments are appropriate for the topic being discussed, and time their statements properly and strategically in the flow of the activities. They need to recognize when to make a comment at the beginning of the discussion before the class moves on to another topic, and when to hold off on comments until they can better gauge how well the group will accept their opinions.

> **"Students with poor self-discipline are often not properly oriented to the tasks they are expected to complete, and are easily sidetracked by the people and activities around them."**

Teaching Students to Coordinate Performance

The most direct way of teaching students to coordinate performance is to teach them how to work with other people. By showing them how to work together, they will naturally learn the skills for coordinating their actions with those of adults and classmates. Cooperative activities can be built into almost any kind of instructional lesson or task. Students can team up in games, discussion groups and even in conversations. With young children and with students having problems in attention or cognition, you may need to be more concrete and direct in the approaches you use to help students respond to what is going on around them. You might start with talking through or role playing performance steps as the students are completing them. With older students you may have to focus more on the timing and fluency of actions to overcome being too hesitant or deliberate in behavior. Some specific ways for teaching students to coordinate their behavior include:

— having each member of a group read or tell part of a continuing story,

— asking them to comment on another student's answers,

— using activities or games in which a student's next response is dictated by the actions or moves of other people,

— asking them to signal when their row is ready before being dismissed for recess,

— having them review homework with one or two classmates before leaving for the day, or call a "study buddy" at home. They could discuss how they will schedule their time, share progress reports on their work and give suggestions for doing the next tasks.

The ability to concentrate on the task at hand is another key element of coordinating behavior with ongoing activities. Students with poor self-discipline are often not properly oriented to the tasks they are expected to complete, and are easily sidetracked by the people and activities around them. Teaching students to screen out distractions allows them to maintain a focus on the tasks and activities they are expected to complete. Begin by making sure they understand what is expected of them and how individual performance steps relate to accomplishing the broader task or objective. Show them how to orient themselves and prepare for an activity before starting it. The design of instructional materials and activities can also be a factor in encouraging better concentration, and you can often improve attention by using audio or visual materials, manipulatives, multi-sensory activities, computer-assisted instruction and other approaches.

> **"Personalizing performance is a crucial aspect of self-discipline as it helps students structure their actions in a way that is efficient and effective for them, based on their own learning and performance characteristics."**

Teach techniques for focusing on performance steps, while ignoring extraneous variables:

— teach students to work on one task at a time. Show them how to separate activities with a transition exercise (e.g., record keeping, assignment review, assembling new materials) to give closure on one task and to help them prepare for the next one,

— teach them to work alongside people who will provide good models of concentration and positive study habits,

— teach them to recognize the types of things that can create distractions (e.g., toys, books or papers from other classes) and to remove them from the work area beforehand,

— teach them how to watch for signs that indicate loss of attention (e.g., staring into space, daydreaming), and how to re-focus attention on the task by looking back over their notes or reviewing directions,

— teach them how to re-start an activity after being interrupted so they don't skip steps or have to re-do them.

During any activity, there are a number of things that compete for the students' attention: Friends they want to talk to, other tasks they prefer doing, other assignments they need to complete. Teach students how to develop a schedule for school work and personal activities to cover a class period, a day, a week, or even longer. A key to this approach is showing them how to structure time to complete specific performance steps you have set as instructional objectives. Not surprisingly, this technique is most often applied to homework and other academic tasks, but you can use the same approach to encourage students to participate in classroom discussions, practice conversation or play skills and perform many other activities.

Four steps to time management:

— **determining how time is currently spent** – students list what they do now and how much time they spend on each step or sub-task;

— **estimating time needed to accomplish each step or sub-task** – students typically underestimate the time it takes them to do school tasks and this step helps them gain a more realistic sense of performance demands;

— **preparing a "to do" list** – students develop a list of steps for completing the tasks or activities;

— **scheduling time for completing the items on the "to do" list** – students prepare a timeline for completing individual performance steps and the overall tasks or activities. They then use the schedule to carry out and track their performance.

3. Personalizing Performance

Performance steps for a task or activity are not rigid or inflexible and successful students vary in the ways they organize and coordinate performance. They may pace and shift their behavior to ensure that they meet the external demands of the situation, and to take into account personal factors such as their interest in the material, their understanding of how much time and effort the assignment requires of them, and their ability to maintain attention to the type of tasks or interactions involved. **Personalizing** performance is a crucial aspect of self-discipline as it helps students structure their actions in a way that is efficient and effective for them, based on their own learning and performance characteristics.

How students personalize their performances:

— assessing their limitations and strengths, and applying this knowledge to the demands of the situation,

— interpreting demands in terms of what is required of them,

— considering different ways in which they could complete performance steps and choosing the way that is best suited for them,

— seeking out or structuring environmental conditions that aid their way of completing steps,

— pacing performance to account for personal factors such as fatigue, level of interest and attention.

Students often figure out tricks or shortcuts to pace their actions, or come up with easier or quicker ways to complete individual steps. These techniques help them overcome or compensate for difficulties they have with meeting behavioral demands. During recess, for example, students whose game-playing abilities are less proficient use their skills to support their more talented teammates. Similarly, during class discussions students may participate in a variety of ways, depending on their knowledge of the subject and their verbal skills. Students who are more verbal and outgoing form ideas on the fly by talking them through in front of class. Those who are more reticent or shy think through comments more thoroughly beforehand and refer to notes or their books to avoid having to extemporize. Students who have trouble remembering course material compensate by responding to comments others are making. Those who have difficulty expressing themselves verbally rely on gestures and posture to show involvement in the discussion. In such ways, personalizing performance steps helps students compensate for their shortcomings and draw on their strengths in order to meet behavioral demands.

Teaching Students to Personalize Performance

Teachers of students with sensory or speech impairments or limitations in movement or cognition are well aware that these children have to learn unique and personalized ways of performing even the most basic tasks. But all students, whether disabled or not, benefit from learning their strengths and limitations, and applying this information to their behavior. The procedures you use can be fairly direct, like demonstrating alternative ways to arrange toys on a shelf, computing math facts, remembering the spelling of a word or recalling dates in history. They can be more indirect as well by giving them more latitude in the ways they complete assigned activities and challenging them to generate alternative performance strategies.

Approaches to personalize performance:

— having students come up with their own way of giving a report, such as a verbal presentation, a collage, skit, a poster session,

— showing them how they can use an array of materials and resources to do a science project,

— creating learning centers in which they can choose different types of activities,

— providing individually-paced computer math drills.

Making adaptations or accommodations in a task or activity can help students with particularly difficult steps that impede their progress. These modifications will accomplish the objectives you defined, but should also encourage students to come up with approaches they can manage themselves. This is an especially useful technique with students who display learning or behavior problems that make tasks difficult to complete in the ways that typical students perform them.

Modifications include:

— using books-on-tape, pictures, study notes, or computer programs to supplement a textbook,

— using different testing formats, e.g., in writing, orally, on audio- or videotapes,

— allowing students to highlight answers with markers instead of copying them on paper,

— giving them additional instructional aids and resources to use in math, such as calculators, number lines or counting sticks.

Teach students how to generate their own ways to perform tasks and activities and how to be flexible when accounting for their learning characteristics, preferences or temperament. Ask them to suggest alternative ways to do a particular task or activity, or encourage them to watch one another completing the performance steps. With repetitious tasks like doing worksheets, remembering math facts or studying for a test, show them how to create variety by making a game or a personal contest out of the activity. You could also teach them to incorporate strengths and abilities into their performance by using more non-verbal communication if they are shy, helping others at things they themselves are good at or contributing more actively in tasks that interest them.

Teaching students to manage their performance will provide them with the fundamental elements of self-discipline. As they learn to organize, coordinate and personalize the actions that form the larger patterns of behavior, they will come to exercise a new degree of self-reliance and control over their performance.

> **"Teach students how to generate their own ways to perform tasks and activities and how to be flexible when accounting for their learning characteristics, preferences or temperament."**

Suggestions for Using Worksheet 3

Worksheet 3 can help you prepare a checklist for observing a group or an individual as they complete a task or activity. You can then use the worksheet to record your observations and set objectives for instruction.

Using the Worksheet:

Begin with starting and ending steps

The simplest way to consider the full range of performance steps is to begin with the behaviors that start and end the situation. Typically the first step is what students do to make the transition from the previous activity, and the last step is what they do to prepare for the next activity.

Keep steps in chronological order

Keeping the steps in a more or less chronological order makes it easier to use the checklist to follow along during your observations.

Keep the focus on required behavior

The list of steps indicate behaviors students need to perform to complete the task or activity. A full list will have about eight to fifteen steps.

Make sure the observation list reflects typical behavior

When you observe the behavior of individual students, your object is to compare their behavior to the C-level behavior of their peers in general education settings. Therefore, the checklist you make needs to reflect average behavior, rather than an ideal level of performance.

Use checklist to mark strengths and weaknesses

On the worksheet, simply mark "+" for steps that are done proficiently, and "o" when steps are missed or done poorly. This will allow you to quickly spot areas of difficulty.

Conduct several observations

When observing groups, you get a pretty clear idea of student behavior with just a couple observations. But when you observe a single student, factors such as mood, amount of sleep, daily events, and others can cause significant changes in behavior from day to day. Therefore, it is best to watch the student perform the task or activity at least 3-5 times to get an accurate appraisal of strengths and weaknesses.

Set helpful objectives

The objectives you set should be based on steps that cause students particular or repeated difficulty. Watch for steps that throw students off their routine or lead to problems in subsequent steps.

"Teach them to incorporate strengths and abilities into their performance by using more non-verbal communication if they are shy, helping others at things they themselves are good at or contributing more actively in tasks that interest them."

Worksheet 3 Example

Mr. Elsworth teaches three periods of ninth grade general science at Parkview High School. The students in his classes have a wide range of abilities, and although he keeps lessons aligned to the school's science curriculum, he tries to make accommodations so all his students can do well. This year, instead of scheduling independent time in his classes for students to do lab reports or begin homework, he is using study teams comprised of students of mixed abilities. He believes the diversity of learning styles and motivational levels of team members will provide a structure for students to get their work done and allow the better students to model self-discipline skills and good study habits. So far this year, the study team notion has had mixed results; several of the teams are doing well but some are struggling. He noticed that the poorer teams' lack of organization and direction are affecting the interactions and productivity of the members. Also, the difficulties these students show in working together have had an adverse affect on the teams nearby. He decided to closely observe Alicia's group, one of the weaker teams in his first period class, to see how to help it become more productive and self-disciplined. If he can get this team on track, it will set a positive tone for other groups. It might also give him insights into improving study teams in other science classes as well.

Mr. Elsworth began his investigation of Alicia's group by watching the behavior of the stronger teams to see why their groups work so well. He noted how they listened to directions and got a sense of what the assignment was before they settled into their groups. He also listed things groups did from the start of a study session until they turned in their work. He then prepared a checklist with places to make notes and comments to provide a more formal guide for his observations. He planned his observation to focus on the group's performance and to circulate around the room to oversee the rest of the class.

Over the course of a week and a half, Mr. Elsworth observed the entire sequence of steps on his checklist four times, and was surprised by some of the results. During his first observation, he noticed the group's tendency to start working before they knew what the assignment was. This quickly led to misdirection in student performance and to arguments over what they were to do. During the second and third observations, the group's lack of cooperation became apparent. He saw that some of the students were reluctant to give help to one another almost as if they were competing for a better grade.

In summarizing his finding, Mr. Elsworth defined the following objectives that he thought would help Alicia's group work more cooperatively.

Skills set in following objectives:

— learn to listen to or read directions before starting work,

— learn to handle disagreements without arguing,

— learn to ask neighbors for help and to give help to neighbors,

— learn to coordinate work with others in the group.

Mr. Elsworth feels these objectives will form the basis for a strong intervention for Alicia's group.

Worksheet 3: Observing behavior and setting objectives for instruction.

Name: _Mr. Elsworth_   Date: _October 20_

Student or group: _Alicia's study group_   Grade: _9_

Task or Activity to be the Focus of Instruction: _Working in study groups_

Performance Steps in Activity or Task:	Behavior Observed (+ = skilled, 0 = unskilled):				
	1st	2nd	3rd	4th	5th
Listens to/read directions for the activity	O	O	O	O	
Asks questions about assignment	O	O	O	+	
Gets out books and materials	+	+	–	+	
Goes quietly over to study group	O	+	+	+	
Reviews assignment directions with group members	O	O	O	O	
Plans assignment with group before working on it	O	O	O	O	
Stays on task	+	O	O	O	
Compares progress with partners	+	O	+	+	
Asks for help from partners if needed	O	O	O	+	
Gives help to partners when asked	O	O	O	+	
Resolves disagreements without arguing	O	O	+	O	
Checks work with partners before handing it in	O	O	+	O	
Turns in assignments when requested	+	+	+	+	

Worksheet 3: Observing behavior and setting objectives for instruction.

Name: _____ Date: _____

Student or group: _____ Grade: _____

Task or Activity to be the Focus of Instruction:

Performance Steps in Activity or Task:	Behavior Observed (+ = skilled, 0 = unskilled):				
	1st	2nd	3rd	4th	5th
_____					
_____					
_____					
_____					
_____					
_____					
_____					
_____					
_____					
_____					
_____					
_____					

Chapter 4

Managing Motivation

Self-Discipline and Motivation

In Chapter 3, we saw that analyzing performance tells us what students need to do to complete a task or activity, but it doesn't tell us why they do it — the factors that keep successful students motivated and directed in their behavior. When students study for a test, pay attention to their teacher and take notes on assignments, they are not acting automatically; rather they're responding to a complex set of conditions that give them opportunities to produce a variety of outcomes. Outcomes are a crucial element in self-discipline because they serve as incentives that motivate and energize student behavior. Students direct their actions toward producing outcomes that will be beneficial and avoiding ones they dislike. Outcomes follow directly from performing tasks or activities.

Outcomes resulting from competent performance include:

— earning a passing grade on a test,

— pleasing classmates or oneself,

— receiving praise from teachers or parents,

— gaining an important piece of information about an assignment or topic of interest,

— having the correct answers on a worksheet,

— winning a game,

— feeling confident and satisfied about one's behavior,

— receiving school awards or classroom privileges,

— having friends to talk with.

Of course, not all outcomes are positive. Behavior that is misdirected or lacks competence also results in outcomes, but ones students try to avoid.

Undesired outcomes include:

— failing a test,

— angering classmates or displeasing oneself,

— being reprimanded by teachers or parents,

— lacking important information about an assignment or topic of interest,

— having incorrect answers on an assignment,

— losing a game,

— feeling disappointed or dissatisfied with one's behavior,

— losing school or classroom privileges,

— being ignored or teased by classmates.

As these examples show, outcomes are natural features of the settings in which students display behavior. They go beyond the rewards and privileges students might earn for good behavior to encompass all the internal and external effects their actions have. In order to be successful in school, students must know how to manage their motivation by identifying outcomes that provide incentives for them and connecting these outcomes to competent performance.

66**Many of the problems you see in unmotivated students result from their inability to use outcomes properly.**99

Observing Student Motivation to Determine Instructional Needs

Many of the problems you see in unmotivated students result from their inability to use outcomes properly. They might not understand the outcomes that follow from competent performance or be aware of the link between outcomes and their behavior. They might not know how to focus their behavior on achieving these outcomes, or think the outcomes are worthwhile. As a result of such problems these students don't have the motivation to succeed in school tasks or activities. You can observe the manner in which students manage their motivation by assessing how well they direct their efforts towards attaining outcomes that arise from competent performance.

Do this investigation in three stages

Stage 1: List natural outcomes for the task or activity you are concerned with,

Stage 2: Plan the best way to observe student responses to these outcomes,

Stage 3: Conduct observations and note the outcomes that need the most attention.

Use this approach with a group of students or with an individual. **Worksheet 4** shows the form Ms. Perkins developed to observe a third grade student named Franklin during recess. She wanted to see if his unruly behavior was caused by an inability to manage outcomes. A blank copy of the worksheet is provided to assist with your planning.

Begin the first stage by describing a task or activity to give focus to your instructional planning as explained in Chapter 3. With this task or activity in mind, list outcomes that typically follow from competent performance. The outcomes you describe should be available to every student who performs successfully, not just to those who are brightest or most diligent. Often it's beneficial to use a categorization system to help with identifying outcomes and organizing your list. For example, Mr. Taylor, a tenth grade social studies teacher, used five categories to describe outcomes for participating in his class presentations.

> "Watching successful students engage in the task or activity and talking with them directly are helpful ways to identify outcomes that are particularly motivating."

1. Academic achievement outcomes – outcomes from accomplishing subject matter tasks:

— understanding more about historical events,

— having answers, ideas and suggestions to contribute to discussions,

— being prepared for a project, test or assignment on the material,

— having an easier time with homework

— avoiding having to re-do work that was done incorrectly.

2. Social contact or status outcomes – outcomes from social interactions and rapport:

— being given praise and recognition from me,

— getting support and encouragement from me or classmates when difficulties arise,

— being able to share knowledge, ideas and personal stories with classmates,

— getting chances to get on my "good side,"

— "fitting in" with the group,

— having classmates think of them as smart or someone to go to for help,

— being seen by parents as getting along or doing well in school.

3. Material outcomes – outcomes involving goals students acquire:

— working in same text or workbook as other students,

— having worksheets and tests with passing grades on them to show to parents,

4. Activity outcomes – outcomes from doing things that are enjoyable, satisfying and relaxing:

— being allowed to join in class projects, games and activities,

— being given time to talk with friends or do a preferred task after the discussion,

— being asked to help a classmate with an assignment,

— earning class or school privileges, e.g. taking the attendance book to the office, cleaning marker boards, being in charge of passing out worksheets.

5. Personal control outcomes – outcomes from having the freedom or authority to regulate themselves and others around them:

— being placed in charge of the class if I have to leave the room,

— avoiding reprimands or detention,

— having more of a say in choosing a group to work in later in the period,

— having more free time at home from getting homework done quickly,

— feeling more relaxed and confident about the class from knowing answers and understanding the material.

Worksheet 4 shows how Ms. Perkins used these categories to list outcomes for cooperative play during recess. As you can see, the categories are not clear-cut or exclusive of one another; they are merely a convenient way to identify and group outcomes for later observation. You should make sure the outcomes you list actually serve to motivate typical students and describe them in positive terms unless it's apparent that avoiding an outcome is a predominant factor in student motivation. Watching successful students engage in the task or activity and talking with them directly are helpful ways to identify outcomes that are motivating.

In Stage Two, decide how to observe student reaction to the outcomes on your list. As with observing performance steps, schedule your time so you can watch student responses to each outcomes from three to five times. You can use a variety of procedures to investigate items on your list, including direct observation, videotaping, interviewing students and examining work samples.

When you observe students, rate their responses as Ms. Perkins did on her worksheet. She placed a check in the "Strong" column when Franklin had a marked response to the outcome, or when he responded in a way that was similar to successful students in the group. She placed a check in the "Weak" column when the outcome provoked a deficient or negative response from Franklin, or was opposite to that shown by successful students. And she put a check in the "Neutral" column when the outcome seemed to prompt a mild or neutral response, or if the outcome was not motivating. Ms. Perkins used the "Comments" section of her worksheet to highlight other important things she discovered about Franklin's reaction to outcomes.

What do I watch for when observing outcomes?

It's important to observe your students' responses to outcomes **from their own perspective** because sometimes the things we think are motivating to students do not actually have this effect. Thus, you should base your assessments on what you see them doing, or trying to do, and on what you already know about them. These are some questions to consider when evaluating student reactions to outcomes:

— What outcomes serve as goals for their behavior? Do they direct their behavior toward particular outcomes? Are these the outcomes for competent performance?

— Do they focus on achieving the same outcomes valued by their peers or are there other outcomes they find motivating?

— Do they know how to produce the outcomes, or show awkward or ineffective attempts to gain them?

— Do they direct their behavior toward outcomes they can't realistically achieve or enjoy?

— Do they know how to sustain their behavior to attain the outcomes, or "give up" when the task becomes difficult or tedious?

— Do they keep particular outcomes in mind while performing the task or activity, or lose sight of their goal?

— Do they attribute the outcomes to the effects of their behavior? Do they recognize the connections between what they do and what happens to them?

— Do they neglect longer term outcomes in favor of immediate gratification?

— Do they show pleasure when they achieve the outcomes, and concern or disappointment when they fail to achieve them?

— Do they value competing or counterproductive outcomes instead of ones for competent performance?

Defining Instructional Objectives

When you complete your observation, summarize your findings in terms of outcomes that have the greatest potential for improving student motivation. Choose as objectives three to five single outcomes or groups of outcomes that would be helpful in increasing incentive when students learn to manage them effectively. Select outcomes that represent strengths and teach them to link them to competent behavior that provides an incentive boost. Remember, students will also benefit greatly from learning to manage outcomes that are now areas of weakness for them, especially when these weak outcomes are strong motivators for successful students. By teaching students to understand and value outcomes that haven't created strong incentive for them in the past, you bring about a more profound change in their behavior than by just working with their strengths. Therefore, pick a mixture of weak and strong outcomes to serve as objectives for instruction.

> "Accessing outcomes requires knowing how to select appropriate ones as goals for performance, how to direct behavior toward producing them, and how to use and enjoy the outcomes when they take place."

The following objectives were defined for Franklin:

— learn to derive motivation from finding out more about game rules and playing techniques,

— learn to derive motivation from gaining a sense of camaraderie with teammates,

— learn to derive motivation from sharing in the fun of the game,

— learn to derive motivation from bringing his own toys and play equipment to share during recess and

— learn to derive motivation from the chance of being team captain or score keeper.

The first objective resulted from her observation that Franklin had a strong desire to play to the ability level of his teammates, and she thinks he would become more cooperative if he realized that getting along better would help him become a better player. She listed the next two objectives but rated them "weak." She observed that Franklin didn't understand that playing cooperatively would improve teammate responses to him, and "having fun" was something he could accomplish in a group activity. If she could strengthen Franklin's response to these outcomes, she felt it would increase his desired to cooperate. She defined the last two objectives because Franklin clearly liked leadership roles, like being in charge of equipment; she will try to teach him that these roles follow naturally from being cooperative.

Teaching Skills for Managing Motivation

Most approaches to discipline address the topic of outcomes in terms of rewards and incentives teachers administer to their students. But viewing outcomes as an area that students must learn to manage themselves allows you to shift your efforts from carrot-and-stick methods to instructional lessons that teach students how to use outcomes to set goals that generate incentive for competent behavior. To use outcomes effectively, students must learn three important self-discipline skills: **Accessing**, **Recognizing** and **Valuing outcomes**. Each skill is crucial in helping students generate interest, energy and perseverance to perform competently in school.

1. Accessing Outcomes

Accessing outcomes is knowing how to produce outcomes that are available for competent performance, and take advantage of them when they occur.

Successful students display this self-discipline skill by:

— selecting outcomes for competent performance as goals for their behavior,

— setting up or creating conditions that make these outcomes more likely to occur,

— carrying out the actions that produce these outcomes,

— sustaining behavior until the outcomes result,

— participating in and enjoying the outcomes once they have obtained them.

> **"Many students who show problems in self-discipline have little or no experience with outcomes for competent performance because their inappropriate actions have prevented their access to them."**

Accessing outcomes includes abilities that go beyond academic, social, and study skills we normally associate with school behavior. It requires knowing how to select outcomes as goals for performance, how to direct behavior toward producing them, and how to use and enjoy the outcomes when they take place. For example, a teacher might let students play computer games with a classmate if they finish their assignments on time. To achieve this outcome, students must know how to do the work she assigns, which requires an understanding of subject matter concepts and the ability to carry out assigned tasks. But in order for computer time to actually motivate students to do their work, they must also understand how to set it as a goal for their behavior, how to get assignments done fast enough to be awarded the time, and how to exercise restraint in talking with neighbors so the time is not withdrawn if they become too noisy or inattentive. Moreover, to fully enjoy and appreciate computer time when they do earn it, the students would have to be skilled at operating a computer, following game rules, and socializing properly with classmates they play with. Without these skills for accessing computer time, the outcome would not have motivating effects on their behavior regardless of their academic skills.

"Recognizing outcomes is understanding the connection between competent performance and the outcomes that follow naturally from this behavior."

Teaching students to access outcomes

Students must know how to use their abilities, talents and resources to produce outcomes, and when they lack key academic or social skills for doing so, you need to develop these skills as part of your instructional lessons. In some cases these basic skills will be the same as those you focus on in your lessons for improving performance, as outlined in Chapter 3, so your procedures may already account for the needed skills. For example, in teaching students how to complete independent work, you also show them how to access outcomes they didn't obtain before, such as feeling pride in finishing their work and earning passing grades. Your procedures for teaching students how to access outcomes may simply involve highlighting the fact that they are able to produce positive outcomes now that their behavior is improving. But many students who show problems in self-discipline have little or no experience with outcomes for competent performance because their inappropriate actions have prevented their access to them. Without this experience, students have no reason to think outcomes are worth trying to produce. You can make outcomes for competent performance more meaningful to students by structuring situations where students receive these outcomes so they experience using and enjoying them. For example, give more assignments or quizzes than you normally do, but make them shorter, so students have opportunities to finish assignments and earn good grades on them. Encourage students to give more greetings to classmates to gain peer acceptance, or praise them when they act appropriately so they receive more teacher attention.

Other ways to teach students to access outcomes:

— have them suggest outcomes they enjoy, like winning a game, and show them how to obtain them,

— pair them with classmates to assist them in participating in recess activities, gym exercises or math drills,

— use things students already enjoy doing, such as coloring or talking with friends, as outcomes for following directions or doing assignments,

— give them variety in the types of things they can work for besides getting passing grades or teacher praise,

— incorporate games, contests and other things students like to do in your daily lessons.

In situations where it's important to build motivation quickly, reduce or alter requirements students must meet in order to access outcomes. By requiring a little less from students, you help them attain outcomes they couldn't produce otherwise. Use this approach when students lack the ability to complete tasks or when it's important to improve their incentive while you work on other instructional areas. For example, when teaching students how to avoid homework by getting assignments done on time, begin by assigning fewer questions to answer, shorter passages to write or fewer pages to read. Modifying requirements increases student incentive to do more work. But this approach is only a temporary, stop-gap measure. You should still challenge them to improve behaviors and should eliminate the adjustments as they increase productivity.

2. Recognizing Outcomes

To become motivated, students must see a direct and personal link between what they do and what results from their behavior. **Recognizing** outcomes is understanding the connection between competent performance and naturally occurring outcomes and using this knowledge to guide their behavior.

Successful students recognize outcomes by:

— identifying outcomes available to them in the performance setting for both competent and incompetent behavior,

— connecting specific outcomes to competent performance, especially ones they see as desirable,

— watching for opportunities to produce outcomes for competent performance,

— keeping the connection between competent performance and desired outcomes in mind while carrying out tasks and activities,

— delaying gratification until they have met the requirements for competent performance.

Successful students stay alert to available outcomes and intuitively link them to their behavior. They strive to personalize and broaden outcomes by making their own games or challenges out of a situation, by seeking extra measures of attention and support from those around them and by using other strategies for increasing their enjoyment and satisfaction. This connection between competent behavior and outcomes helps students sustain their behavior through the entire sequence of performance steps and keeps them focused on outcomes they desire. This focus, along with the strategies they have learned for delaying gratification aids them in working towards long term, and desirable outcomes. For example, students successful at interacting with peers recognize that having friends and being accepted in groups requires certain behavior. They know they must compromise their feelings, tone down their opinions on sensitive topics, and sometimes give in on their preferences about what they would like to do. This recognition may be implicit — they may not be able to say what behaviors they use or what outcomes they seek — but it is a driving force in their motivation. As a result, successful students have a keen, if unspoken, sense of the terrors that await them if they break peer taboos, as well as the satisfaction and status they gain from building friendships with competent social interactions.

Teaching students to recognize outcomes

You can improve student recognition of outcomes by having them identify ones for competent performance before they begin an activity. This approach makes the required behavior more meaningful and functional for them so they can use these outcomes as goals and incentives for behavior. For example, before you have students begin an assigned task, discuss how getting the work done will help them learn the material, get better grades and earn extra time to play with friends after school. Encourage the class to periodically re-state these outcomes when their attention begins to wander. A more formal approach for improving recognition is showing students how to prepare a "performance contract" that explains which outcomes result from behaviors like coming to class on time, following school rules, turning in homework or getting along with playmates. The contract describes outcomes students desire and lists steps to earn them. Such contracts serve as a reminder of the outcomes and a guide in carrying out the required behavior.

> "Valuing outcomes is knowing how to assign worth to outcomes for competent performance and how to compare this worth to that of other outcomes which might be available to them."

> **"Students who have difficulty with self-discipline often fail to follow the lead of those around them in setting value on outcomes for competent performance. They don't see the advantages of acting competently and make no effort to align their desires with the demands of the setting. They may even value outcomes that are counter-productive."**

Other ways to teach outcome recognition:

— post class rules along with rewards and privileges students can earn by following them,

— give periodic reminders of benefits of asking for help, waiting one's turn, cleaning up a work area or playing by the rules,

— link a consistent set of rewards, such as earning free time or bonus points, to regularly assigned tasks so outcomes become a predictable part of the routine,

— have the class create a list of outcomes from doing homework, completing an art project or practicing math facts, and emphasize those that are most functional and enjoyable to students,

— reduce delays between students' turning in assignments and giving them grades or praise so they receive more immediate feedback for their efforts.

When students have difficulty working toward long term outcomes, teach them how to set intermediate outcomes to mark their progress toward the delayed ones. This approach makes these types of outcomes a more tangible part of competent performance. For example, teach your class how to break long term rewards — such as a Friday pizza party — into smaller increments and track daily progress so the party seems attainable. Improve student understanding of how daily work relates to semester grades by showing them how to make their own report cards that summarize how each day's efforts affect their grades. Supplement daily reports by suggesting strategies that lead to better grades. You could also enlist the aid of classmates by having them give each other prompts to bolster the approach even further.

If you suspect that students fail to link outcomes to their behavior because they underestimate their abilities or lack the confidence to use them, focus on showing them they do have needed skills and talents. Center your procedures on giving them a truer picture of their ability to produce outcomes, or highlighting important sources of support they can draw on for assistance. For example, students who are reluctant to join games: You can help them overcome their hesitation by showing them they do have the skills needed to participate. For example, help them understand their capabilities by listing requisites for playing in recess. Or show a video of game-playing activities and discuss the skills involved. Direct the activity toward demonstrating that they have or can acquire the necessary skills and talents.

Sometimes students have difficulty recognizing outcomes because they are overshadowed by negative outcomes they're trying to avoid. They don't consider the benefits of their behavior because they focus on other results — real or imagined — that they view as unpleasant or intimidating. In such cases, teach students how to prevent negative outcomes from occurring or reduce their aversive effects. For example, you may have students who don't do assignments because they are embarrassed by the number of times they have to ask for help. Reduce their sense of embarrassment by teaching them to choose someone to ask who won't criticize them and who is able to provide the help without their having to ask for it.

3. Valuing Outcomes

Students must see outcomes as desirable or "worth the effort" before they will use them as incentives for behavior. **Valuing** outcomes is knowing how to assign worth to outcomes for competent performance and to compare this worth to that of the other outcomes available to them.

Successful students value outcomes by:

— looking for and seeking out opportunities to produce outcomes for competent performance,

— performing difficult, tedious, boring or long-term tasks to obtain them,

— placing them as higher priorities for their behavior than more immediate or easier-to-obtain outcomes,

— associating, combining or linking these outcomes with other outcomes to generate greater incentive,

— showing positive emotion when they produce them and negative emotion when they fail to do so.

Successful students know how to align their desires with outcomes for competent performance and actively seek out such outcomes as pleasing their teachers and classmates, earning privileges, getting good grades and participating in new learning experiences. Furthermore, they have learned to value outcomes like these to the extent that they will follow classroom rules, comply with teacher directions, do assignments, and meet other requirements that involve great amounts of effort and attention. Students do these things because they believe the benefits they get from them are worth their time and energy. These benefits establish the value or worth of outcomes, which help students stay focused on assigned tasks and ignore the gratification that comes from outcomes of lesser value. Students learn to set value on outcomes quite naturally by watching for cues in the environment. Everything from classroom rules and regulations to the comments of other students give indications of how they should view outcomes.

Teaching students to value outcomes

Students who have difficulty with self-discipline often fail to follow the lead of those around them in setting value on outcomes for competent performance. They don't see the advantages of acting competently and as a result, make no effort to control their desires or align them with the demands of the setting. At the same time, they may value outcomes that are counterproductive — like getting attention for inappropriate behavior — and work in opposition to competent performance. With students like these, stress the importance, benefits and worth of outcomes from competent performance. Highlight positive results of working hard, doing their best and sticking to difficult tasks. Call their attention to instances in which they benefited from being courteous, obeying the rules or following teacher directions. Present personal stories to show that taking the "easier way out" may seem attractive and at first, but resulted in less beneficial or undesirable consequences in the long run.

Other ways to help students value outcomes:

— call attention to how a classmate they admire enjoys earning free time or showing a "B" paper to another teacher,

— link desired with less desired outcomes, like assigning a friendly partner to help on difficult tasks, or showing them how to make a game of reviewing spelling words or making up sentences,

— create more novelty, variety and interest by periodically changing privileges and rewards, seating arrangements or grading procedures,

— give more exposure and recognition to non-preferred outcomes, like cleaning up the play area, so students have a reason to feel proud of their work, gain peer acceptance or earn teacher praise.

The value students place on outcomes is related to the experiences they have with them. Students don't value outcomes they have not experienced; and if they do give them value, it may be distorted. Arrange for students to gain more experience with certain outcomes to learn they are satisfying and worthwhile. For example, some students may not value your praise because they think this kind of attention is "for babies." But they may have had little experience with receiving praise, since their behavior tends to bring them in conflict with adults. To teach them to place more value on this outcome, use activities they enjoy as a context for giving attention, like helping you arrange materials for class, grade papers or go with you on errands. Perhaps then they will come to view your praise during class time as a desired experience and be willing to act properly to gain even more of it.

Sometimes the repeated reprimands a teacher gives students for being out of their seats, talking back, or not doing their work has diminished the rapport she could have had with them. Poor rapport negates the value of teacher-centered outcomes such as praise, grades and privileges, and makes students less willing to align their values with yours. Strengthening the rapport you have with students teaches them to value outcomes for competent performance, because it allows you to play a significant role in developing their skills. Build rapport by using non-confronting techniques to encourage their behavior. Instead of reprimanding them for being off-task, re-direct them to their work by pointing out the next steps to complete or by reminding them of outcomes they can produce by getting back on task. Structure work times so students don't have occasion to leave their seats by having groups share supplies and materials, or directing questions and problems to a designated member who asks the teacher for help. At the same time, supplement these procedures by inviting students to join you in individual or small group tasks they enjoy, by asking for their input in choosing activities, by getting to know them better on a personal level, and by increasing the number of positive, non-judgmental interactions you have with them. By building rapport in these ways, you increase student desire to follow your suggestions and wishes, and make them more receptive to valuing the outcomes you promote.

A final approach for teaching students to value outcomes is to link them to **artificial rewards**. Artificial rewards are outcomes, such as special privileges, stickers, tokens, and other tangible or edible items that aren't normally associated with competent performance. They can be powerful tools for increasing student incentive when students are resistant to outcomes for competent performance. Offering artificial rewards as a temporary component of your teaching increases students' incentive enough to enlist their participation in the lesson. The key to making this approach work is linking rewards as closely as possible with the natural outcomes you're promoting. As students build proficiency in behavior and earn rewards, emphasize natural outcomes by stressing their benefits. Establishing this link is crucial to the success of teaching self-discipline because students must learn to shift their attention to natural outcomes to make permanent changes in their behavior.

Motivation is a driving force for competent behavior — it makes performance purposeful and worthwhile. Teaching students how to manage motivation promotes their sense of self-direction and self-efficacy because it gives them the ability to influence and control conditions for obtaining outcomes they desire. As you teach students to access, recognize and value outcomes for competent performance, they begin to align their behavior to school demands not because they have to but because they want to.

Suggestions for Using Worksheet 4

Worksheet 4 helps you develop a checklist to observe how students manage their motivation. Use the worksheet to record observations and set objectives for teaching lessons. Suggestions for using the worksheet include:

Watch for effects of student behavior

Outcomes are the results of competent behavior, so look for the effect student actions have on the environment. Some of these will be immediate but others might be delayed, such as a teacher praising students later in the day for playing well during recess.

Describe outcomes in positive terms

Describe outcomes positively unless avoiding an outcome should be a key element in student motivation. List outcomes they receive rather than avoid because they are usually more concrete and easier to teach in your lessons.

Outcomes can be internal or external

Sometimes internal outcomes will be more powerful incentives for behavior than peer- or teacher-based outcomes. Watch carefully for reactions or signs of emotion that result from student behavior.

List outcomes for typical students

Usually the outcomes that only the brightest and most diligent students receive will not be helpful in instructional lessons because they are beyond the reach of other students. Focus on the more conventional outcomes.

View outcomes from students' perspective

Look for outcomes that really motivate student behavior even though they might not be the things you would think of as incentives.

Set objectives to motivate student performance

Objectives that provide a mix of weak and strong outcomes strengthen your lessons. Your objectives should focus on teaching students how to manage outcomes themselves rather than on your administering outcomes to them.

Worksheet 4 Example

Franklin is a student in Ms. Perkins' third grade class. He usually performs well on assignments and other in-class activities, but during recess and free times he's aggressive and bullies classmates. On the playground, when he wants to join games and play on the equipment, he pushes his way into the group and tries to take over and be the center of attention. Franklin is big for his age, well coordinated, and has good play and social skills, but uses unruly and intimidating behavior to gain peer acceptance. Now, classmates exclude him from their play whenever they can, and often complain about him to teachers and supervisors. This makes Franklin frustrated and discouraged and even more prone to becoming aggressive. Recently, the recess problems are carrying over to the classroom and he's having more conflicts with classmates and run-ins with Ms. Perkins. She would like Franklin to learn to play cooperatively to counteract the difficulties he is having socially. She feels other students would look up to him if he would change his approach to playing. The key, she feels, is improving the way he manages motivation because he doesn't realize his actions are a barrier to the peer attention and status he's seeking.

Ms. Perkins decided to focus her investigation on game playing activities during recess since this is when he has the most difficulty interacting. She observed the cooperative play of students who do well in small group situations to see what types of outcomes motivate them to get along with playmates. She prepared a list of outcomes they produce with their behavior and watched how they managed them. She saw, for example, that they direct behavior toward outcomes like getting along and having fun even when they don't necessarily enjoy the activity or get their way. And they place a high value on new learning skills and play techniques as well as on being part of a harmonious group.

Ms. Perkins listed the outcomes from play activities on her worksheet and observed how Franklin reacted to them during group play. Over the course of several days, she checked each item based on whether he showed a strong, weak or neutral reaction to the outcome. As she suspected, Franklin showed a strong competitive desire to play as well as his peers even when he didn't understand the rules or skills involved. He also seemed to enjoy new game activities and the toys other students brought to recess. She was surprised to see, though, that "just having fun" wasn't as strong a motivation with him as it was with the other children.

She described her findings in terms of these four objectives:

— learning to derive motivation from finding out more about game rules and skills,

— learning to derive motivation from a sense of camaraderie with teammates,

— learning to derive motivation from sharing in the fun of the game,

— learning to derive motivation from bringing his own toys and play equipment to share during recess.

Ms. Perkins plans to develop instructional lessons to teach Franklin how to use these outcomes as incentives for cooperating better with his playmates.

Worksheet 4: Observing outcomes and setting objectives for instruction.

Name: Ms. Perkins	Date: October 27
Student or group: Franklin	Grade: 3

Task or Activity to be the Focus of Instruction: Group play activities during recess

Outcomes Resulting from Activity:	Outcomes Observed (s = strong w = weak n = neutral)				
	1st	2nd	3rd	4th	5th
Achievement Outcomes:					
Learning more about game rules and playing techniques	s	s	n	s	
Social Contact/Status Outcomes:					
Getting praise from playing well	n	s	s	n	
Gaining a sense of camaraderie from teammates	w	w	w	n	
Sharing in the fun of the group	w	w	w	w	
Having classmates to pal around with going to and from class	s	n	s	s	
Impressing other students with play skills	s	s	s	n	
Materials Outcomes:					
Being in charge of play equipment	s	s	s	n	
Getting chances to bring own toys to share	s	s	s	n	
Being allowed to play with other people's toys	s	n	s	s	
Activity Outcomes:					
Expending physical energy	s	s	s	s	
Having a change of pace from schoolwork					
Playing games and using the playground equipment					
Personal Control Outcomes					
Having a chance to choose the game for the group	n	s	n	s	
Being a team leader once and a while	s	s	s	s	
Suggesting game rules and team strategies	s	n	s	n	
Having more choices in what to play and who to play with	s	s	s	s	

Worksheet 4: Observing outcomes and setting objectives for instruction.

Name: _____ Date: _____

Student or group: _____ Grade: _____

Task or Activity to be the Focus of Instruction:					
Outcomes Resulting from Activity:	**Outcomes Observed** **(s = strong w = weak n = neutral)**				
	1st	**2nd**	**3rd**	**4th**	**5th**

Chapter 5

Managing Judgments

Self-Discipline and Judgments

Up to this point, we have viewed self-discipline as if what's going on when students engage in performance is fixed or static — as though behavior and the outcomes that arise from it are tied to established, predictable conditions in the environment. In reality, this is far from true. In real-life situations, such features as physical surroundings, conditions in the setting, and interactions of peers and adults shift considerably while students perform tasks and activities. Students must remain alert to changing conditions because they require considerable adjustment in performance.

Because environmental conditions are always in flux, successful students continually make judgments about their behavior as they go about daily activities. They maintain a keen awareness of environmental conditions to gear their behavior to what is happening around them. They make constant determinations about which skills to use, when to use them, how strong or complex to make their actions and other related issues. At the same time, they monitor and interpret the effects their behavior is having on their surroundings to evaluate progress in achieving desired outcomes. Even during a casual activity like having a conversation with friends, students make important judgments about their behavior: How to greet one another, what topics to talk about, when to add comments to the discussion and whether to support or criticize someone's opinion. Successful students manage judgments like these to evaluate and adjust their behavior to the demands of the situation.

> **"Because environmental conditions are always in flux, successful students continually make judgments about their behavior as they go about daily activities."**

Observing Student Judgments to Determine Instructional Needs

Judgments are the issues students respond to when directing and regulating their performance. Students who have difficulty managing judgments often fail to read cues in the environment that pertain to these issues. They may not attend to these cues, misinterpret them, or not know how to make needed adjustments in their behavior. During conversations with classmates, for example, these students aren't alert to the make up or mood of the group before they begin talking. They don't attend to the comments, facial expressions and body language of group members to see if their statements are being accepted or provoke anger, ridicule or other negative reactions. They misread what is said to them or not know how to respond to reactions of others to their comments As a result of problems like these, they say or do things that disrupt the flow of interactions or act in ways that cause arguments or hurt feelings.

Investigate problems students have when making judgments in three stages:

Stage 1: List judgments for the task or activity you are concerned with,

Stage 2: Plan the best way to observe how the students manage these judgments,

Stage 3: Conduct observations and note judgments that need attention.

Worksheet 5 shows the format Mrs. Kelly used to investigate the difficulties her seventh graders have managing judgments during conversations with peers in the cafeteria. A blank copy of the worksheet is at the end of the chapter.

In Stage 1, after you choose the activity to give a focus to your investigation, list the judgments that help successful students direct, monitor and regulate their behavior. Your list should account for judgments occurring throughout the entire sequence of performance; as students prepare for the activity, during the activity, and when they have finished it. Pay particular attention to the times when performance demands an adjustment and students need to redirect their behavior. Since students make a variety of determinations during any situation, limit your list of judgments to ones you're most concerned with.

Mr. Baker, a fourth grade teacher, used five categories to help him describe the judgments his successful fourth graders make when studying spelling words for a weekly quiz:

Judgments about the content of performance — decisions about whether student behavior is focused on the spelling assignment that he gave to the class, such as:

— whether students are studying the list of words I assigned for the week,

— whether their list contains all the words that will be on the quiz,

— whether they can read the words on the list.

Judgments about the pacing of performance — decisions about whether student behavior is carried out and timed properly, such as:

— whether they are studying the words in the best order for remembering them,

— whether they are studying enough words each day to prepare for the quiz,

— whether they are keeping up in writing the words while taking the quiz,

Judgments about the quality of performance — decisions about whether student behavior is accurate and precise enough, such as:

— whether they are concentrating enough while practicing to remember the spelling of the words,

— whether they are making mistakes in writing out the words,

— whether their study habits are helpful in remembering most of the words until the quiz,

— whether they are spelling each word correctly during the quiz.

Judgments about the quantity of performance — decisions about whether student behavior is taking place often enough, long enough, or with enough speed, force or animation, such as:

— whether they are studying long enough to remember the words,

— whether they are giving the most difficult words the proper amount of emphasis,

— whether they are writing out or reciting the words enough times to recall them for the quiz,

— whether they have spelled enough words correctly on the quiz to earn a passing grade.

Judgements about the placement of performance — decisions about whether student behavior is situated with regard to environmental conditions, such as:

— whether they are studying when they are supposed to be,

— whether the immediate surroundings are conducive to studying,

— whether they are drawing properly on the resources available for studying, e.g., checking with me or their neighbors when they need help,

— whether they are oriented properly during the quiz so they concentrate on spelling the words and so I don't think they are cheating.

Worksheet 5 shows how Mrs. Kelly used these same categories to describe judgments in her observation of peer conversations.

Plan your observations for students who show problem behavior to evaluate their ability to make each judgment on your list and decide which ones pose the most difficulties. A list of performance steps, as discussed in Chapter 3, can be a very useful guide in identifying judgments that impede competent performance because it allows you to look across the entire task or activity. For example, watch performance steps at the beginning of your list to see how students make judgments about preparing for the task and being in the proper location or orientation to begin. Focus on the middle steps to watch for judgments in the timing and pacing of their behavior, and in aligning and integrating their behavior with that of their classmates. Use the later steps to investigate difficulties in judging the quantity or quality of the work they have completed.

Direct observation is the best procedure to use in your investigation, but you can supplement it with one-on-one interviews, reports from other teachers, review of work samples and other procedures. For example, ask students why they did certain things to evaluate whether they were attending to proper environmental conditions and interpreting them correctly. To keep track of assessment results, devise a check sheet like the one Mrs. Kelly used with her students. **Worksheet 5** shows how on the left side of the worksheet, she listed judgments that might pose a problem for students and ones she wanted to gain more information about. On the right side, she made a column for each time she observed her students. During her observations, she used "+'s" to denote the judgments she saw the students make correctly and "O's" to mark judgments they didn't make effectively, either because they failed to make the judgment or responded to it incorrectly. She also added a "Comments" section to the worksheet to elaborate on important things she discovered about the students' ability to manage judgments during their conversations.

What to Watch for When Observing Students

As you conduct observations, watch whether students make the same judgments about their performance, and at the same points in the sequence, as successful students do, and whether they act correctly based on these decisions. Make this determination by comparing the judgments they make to those successful students make under the same conditions. These are some questions to help you evaluate student behavior:

— Do students attend to environmental conditions when they plan and carry out their behavior? Do they react properly to conditions that indicate what to do and when to do it? Are there conditions they ignore or misinterpret?

— Do they align their behavior with these conditions? Is their behavior carried out at the right times, directed toward the right people and performed in the right locations?

— Do they adjust their behavior when changes in performance conditions or available outcomes occur? When they see that conditions have changed, do they know what the change means?

— Do they alter their behavior when their actions are ineffective or inappropriate? Do they use a different approach when their actions are not successful?

— Do they remain fairly rigid from one performance opportunity to the next even though the circumstances are different?

— Do they misjudge the overall proficiency of their behavior, e.g., do they act as if they have done better (or worse) than they actually did?

Defining Instructional Objectives

When you complete your observation, summarize the results in terms of the three to five judgments that will have the greatest effect on improving student behavior **if they learn to manage them more effectively**. The following are objectives Mrs. Kelly set for students to help improve conversations in the cafeteria:

— learn to judge whether they are listening closely to what others are saying,

— learn to judge whether it's the appropriate time to make a comment,

— learn to judge whether to continue talking on a topic or to change to a new topic,

— learn to judge whether their comments and body language are showing the proper support or sensitivity to another person's feelings.

She defined the first two objectives because many students misjudged how much attention they needed to give to their conversations. They seemed to lose their sense of what their friends were saying because they got distracted by other things, like another conversation going on across the table. As a result, they made comments that didn't fit in with the discussion or didn't realize the group had gone on to a different topic. She included the third objective because students had difficulty judging how long to keep on a particular topic. Sometimes they shifted topics before the group was ready to move on; sometimes they stayed with a topic too long ignoring disinterested looks. She added the fourth objective because some students didn't realize how insensitive their comments were and hurt friends' feelings unintentionally.

Teaching Skills for Managing Judgments

Teach students to manage judgments and show them how to use information or cues coming from the environment to make decisions about their behavior. On a fundamental level, teacher-directed comments and suggestions about their performance can give them much guidance, but there are other kinds of information they must learn to use as well. Information arises from such sources as the physical surroundings, other students in the setting, ongoing activities and the students' own responses, internal senses and feelings.

Students can judge how they're doing by looking to the following cues:

— teacher's comments, tone of voice, facial expressions and gestures,

— notes and examples written on the marker board or in textbooks,

— answers other students give to the teacher's questions,

— comments neighbors whisper about the material,

— things they recall from readings or yesterday's class discussion,

— feelings of frustration or satisfaction with work they're doing.

These and other sources of information help students judge whether they are learning the material, giving the correct answers and performing competently in other ways — if they know how to use the information these sources provide. You can see from these examples that information for judging performance comes from natural features of the setting. It goes beyond evaluative comments you might give and encompasses all internal and external sources of information students use to judge their actions. **Three** self-discipline skills enable students to use information to manage their judgments: **Attending** to information, **interpreting** information and **applying** information. By teaching these skills, you give students the ability to monitor and adjust their behavior so it is aligned to the environment around them.

> *"Attending doesn't mean paying attention to all environmental cues available, but involves looking for information when it's really needed to make important determinations about behavior."*

1. Attending to Information

The most fundamental aspect of managing judgments is the ability to attend to information. **Attending** doesn't mean paying attention to all environmental cues available, but involves looking for information when it is actually needed to make an important determination about behavior.

Successful students attend to information by:

— recognizing when they need information to make a judgment about their behavior,

— filtering important information from extraneous or redundant information,

— looking for information to guide in structuring behavior and in deciding when and how to perform the actions,

— watching for information to evaluate what they have done so far, or to determine what they should do next,

— monitoring ongoing information in deciding whether to maintain, adjust or end behavior,

— watching for information to judge the overall effectiveness of their behavior, and for planning what to do with the next performance opportunities.

When successful students hold conversations, they take an inventory of the people in the group before starting to talk with them. During conversations they attend to the comments, facial expressions and body language to see if their statements are being accepted, or if they provoke anger, ridicule or other negative reactions. They notice when others are listening or are distracted, and are quick to pick up on new arrivals or other unexpected events that dictate a change in language, topic or mannerism. At the end of the interaction, they evaluate what happened with their performance for future reference. Knowing which information sources to look to and when to watch for them is an important aspect of this process because students do not need to pay attention to everything around them. With assignments, for example, they listen to teacher directions only until they understand her expectations. They only glance at the clock one or two times to evaluate their progress, look at their neighbor only when they come to the end of a section, or check to see if the teacher is close when they need to ask her a question.

Teaching Students to Attend to Information

The most direct approach for teaching students to attend to information is to alert them to important cues in the environment and show them how to use them. Emphasize cues they can use to assess their readiness for activities by using the same signals each time, such as standing in front of the room and saying "Class, today we will . . ." Highlight conditions under which students make decisions by making them more prominent, like clapping your hands, underlining key words or giving directions in small increments. If you are teaching students how to judge whether their comments are relevant, point out reactions students normally receive depending on whether their comments are relevant or not. These reactions might include your facial expressions and gestures, the remarks of other students or a sudden stillness in the room. Use a video of class discussions to highlight reactions like these and help students practice identifying them. By using cues in these ways, students are able to judge for themselves whether they are on the right topic and to adjust their behavior accordingly.

Other ways to teach students to attend:

— have them describe to one another the cues they use to decide whether they are successful in conversations, small group discussions or oral presentations,

— give them a sample craft or art project to use to guide decisions about what to do next,

— let them exchange book reports and show them how to judge whether the work fits a predefined set of guidelines,

— have them underline or use markers to highlight aspects of math computation they need to be especially careful with,

— have them color code storage areas for toys or supplies so they can decide where things go,

— teach them to pause briefly after asking a question and getting an answer in order to judge whether the answer they receive addresses their question or helps them proceed with an assignment.

"Interpreting information involves reading environmental cues correctly and understanding how they relate to performance."

Students often have difficulty judging their performance because they fail to attend to information frequently enough. They may start assignments with the group, but get off-task because they fail to judge the pace of their performance. Teaching students to make frequent evaluations of their progress by using sub-tasks or benchmarks can focus their attention directly on required activities. For example, have students judge the pace of their work by checking with a neighbor after every five questions and ask for help if they fall behind. Have them mark their worksheet with time estimates for when they should complete individual sections and check the clock when they finish each segment. Or show them how to do practice quizzes to judge their progress in preparing for a test.

Some students depend too much on others to judge their behavior, rather than attending to cues that enable them to do it themselves. They wait for a teacher's approval before continuing their work, or they don't consider the effects their behavior has on classmates until someone points them out. Have students keep a record of their performance and the reactions they see around them. Record keeping is a beneficial tool because it gives students a concrete measure of how they are doing. It can be done by making X's on a workbook page for each problem they complete, or through each compliment they give another student, or by making graphs, charts, notes in a log book and entries in a journal. For example, they can keep a log of teacher directions they carry out, disagreements they resolve successfully, the number of pages they read, or sections of a report they complete. They can then use these measures to judge the progress of their behavior and make adjustments accordingly.

2. Interpreting Information

Attending to information does not ensure accurate judgments of behavior; students must also be able to interpret information they receive. **Interpreting** information involves reading environmental cues correctly and understanding how they relate to performance.

Successful students interpret information by:

— using the information to develop an effective course of action,

— making adjustments in behavior based on how the environment reacts to their performance,

— judging the effectiveness of their performance from behavioral effects, standards and guidelines,

— deciding what to do next using observed behavioral results and outcomes.

When students talk to one another during lunchtime, the determinations they make about their behavior depend on their ability to interpret information correctly. Successful students decide what to talk about by assessing friends' comments and reactions. They know from the tone of the conversation and looks on peers' faces whether they should joke or be serious, whether they should talk or listen, and whether they should be teasing or supportive. Knowing how to interpret information also helps students understand their own behavior and its effects. When successful students work on assignments, they know from the tone of the teacher's voice or her expression if she is pleased with their behavior and they adjust their behavior accordingly. They can judge from the work of peers how well they are progressing, when they are getting stuck or spending too long on a problem. They know from comments of classmates if their understanding of the material is more or less advanced than average. Reading information in these ways is essential to meeting the demands of the situation.

Teaching Students to Interpret Information

Students who have difficulty interpreting information tend to make wrong judgments about their performance. They may not react properly to cues for what to do and when to do it, their behavior may be misdirected, or they may misjudge the overall proficiency of their behavior and think they have done better (or worse) than they actually did. A useful approach for helping these students interpret information is to show them how to respond more deliberately to circumstances around them, rather than reacting through impulse. One technique is a "stop action" procedure in which students pause at certain points in their performance to review what they have done before continuing. This procedure teaches them how to make mental adjustments in behavior based on environmental reactions and effects before they commit to a particular course of action. This approach also encourages students to think through outcomes they are trying to achieve and judge whether their responses will further their aims.

Other ways to interpret information:

— ask them to figure out what steps come next in a science experiment based on what they have done so far, or on what the final result should be,

— have them role play different social interactions, like handling a disagreement or changing the opinion of a group, and ask them to suggest options and the probable results,

— provide them with examples and non-examples of a concept, like democracy, and show them how to judge which ones fit the attributes of the concept,

— show a video of various conversational styles and ask students to judge which would be the more effective in accomplishing a particular aim, like borrowing a school supply, asking for more time with an assignment, or getting help with a project,

— have them observe a play activity and show them how to read the circumstances before approaching the group with a request to play.

"Applying information is the ability to use cues from the environment to develop and carry out an effective course of action."

Some students fail to take into account the full range of conditions before beginning their performance or fail to weigh changes that take place in these conditions. Teach these students how to assess performance conditions to judge their behavior correctly. For example, students often get into arguments during class discussions because they misinterpret responses of classmates, viewing their comments as condescending or critical instead of helpful. Have the class prepare guidelines for having discussions so everyone understands how to interact ahead of time. Demonstrate how people often use key terms and voice patterns to communicate their intentions, and that these are usually important indicators of a person's reactions. Or have students discuss the merits of giving one another "the benefit of the doubt" until they clarify the person's intentions.

Students sometimes misperceive environmental cues because they fail to differentiate between relevant and extraneous information. You see this when students work in groups and give each other mixed signals about getting back on task after someone makes a personal or off-task comment. They may tell one another to get back to work but at other times draw each other even further off task. Teach the students who have difficulty responding to the subtleties of the group's actions to interpret the cues more accurately. For example, you could show them how to ignore off-task comments or to use redirection to get the group working again. Or suggest that each group designate a peer monitor to keep track of behavior so students learn to judge more clearly when they get off-task.

Sometimes, you may need to teach students to use multiple sources of information to make the meaning of information clearer. This approach is useful when a single information source provides incomplete or inconsistent information, like when students rely too heavily on their own perceptions of how they are doing. You often see students on the playground or in gym arguing with teammates because they have an unrealistic view of their playing abilities. They may see their actions as better coordinated or more central to their team's efforts than they really are and naturally take offense when someone criticizes their play or offers suggestions. Teach these students to be more open to teammates' suggestions by showing how winning depends on team efforts rather than individual play. Add that judgments about their own play should be based on how well the team works together. Stress advantages of being explicit and diplomatic in giving suggestions and in using suggestions to judge playing techniques. Encourage teams to choose a referee to make the final determination in team disputes. Perhaps these multiple sources of information like these will help students make better judgments about their play.

3. Applying Information

Attending to and interpreting information are crucial self-discipline skills, but but they are of little use without the ability to turn this knowledge into clear plans for performance. **Applying** information is the ability to use cues from the environment to develop and carry out an effective course of action.

Successful students apply information by:

— using information to anticipate situational demands and expectations, and to prepare ahead of time to meet them,

— employing information to develop response patterns that have a good chance of being successful,

— monitoring cues so behavior begins and stays aligned with activities and interactions,

— using cues in adapting to changes in performance conditions,

— using behavioral results to work out alternative response patterns when the first attempts at performance are unsuccessful or inefficient,

— drawing on cues or characteristics of previous performance opportunities to plan future behavior.

Successful students use environmental cues to anticipate the demands of a situation and make the needed preparations. When they meet friends in the hallway, they're ready to use the right greetings and gestures based on their assessment of the circumstances. If they notice their friends reacting negatively to something they say, they immediately find ways to modify or clarify their statements. If their friends seem uninterested in what they are saying, they find a new topic or defer to someone else. Sometimes they have to make these kinds of adjustments several times before finding the right thing to say or smoothing over an awkward moment. But by constantly redirecting their behavior in reaction to cues, successful students ensure their words and actions stay in line with ongoing demands of the situation.

Applying information also involves planning future behavior. Students use information to review and evaluate their actions so they can improve or refine them in the future. When successful students complete an assignment, they reflect on how well they did. They note how long it took them to finish the work, find out if others did it differently and compare the approach they used with others they have used before. They reflect on the comments and non-verbal reactions they received from the teacher — especially if she was pleased (or displeased) with what they were doing. Based on the information from these sources, they determine whether they need to change their behavior by working faster next time, reading directions more carefully, asking more questions, or making other adjustments. Much of this process is informal, but it's essential in making effective use of information.

Teaching Students to Apply Information

Students who have difficulty applying information realize that actions are wrong but don't know what to do about it. They listen to directions for an assignment but don't know how to begin. They notice a shift in a class discussion but don't know how to adjust to it. They know they made a mistake in responding to their teacher but aren't able to correct it. A straightforward way of teaching them to apply information is to give them practice in following up on the judgments they make. If they have correctly judged that their behavior is correct, teach them to continue with their performance. If they realize they have made a mistake, show them how to review and adjust their actions by trying other performance options or seeking assistance. For example, during class discussions when students see they have lost concentration, teach them to check with their neighbors, review board notes or ask you or a classmate to repeat what was just said. Have them plan ahead for different contingencies that might arise. For example, if students fail to correct simple mistakes before turning their work in, review ahead of time the errors they could make on an assignment and have them develop strategies for avoiding or correcting them. Then, as they review their work and judge that an answer is probably wrong, they correct their errors on their own.

Other procedures for applying information:

— give students samples that show how to check their spelling or writing style and to correct errors,

— use problem situations, like misplacing homework or losing lunch money, and have them develop behavioral solutions,

— set up a study buddy or homework hotline program to use when they need help with assignments,

— have them observe playmates showing good sportsmanship and show them how to use these techniques during games,

— teach them how to take risks, like asking someone for a date, by using skits or other supportive or non-threatening activities,

— provide a drop box for them to suggest situations or interactions they have difficulty with and use their ideas to role play behavioral options.

Some students don't know how to adjust their behavior after making a judgment because they're confused or overwhelmed by the number of choices they have. They may deliberate so long in choosing a way to ask for help, to join a play group or respond to a classmate's criticism, that they miss the opportunity to respond at all. In situations when almost any of the options they choose will be correct, teach them to make a choice quickly and to go on with their performance. For example, show them how successful students use the same responses to ask for help, join a play group, or react to criticism. Teach them how to select from a set of options based on considerations like which alternative is the most likely to succeed, or which is the quickest, easiest or most comfortable for them to use. For example, use class discussions or peer suggestions to help students to generate additional options, or set up simulations and role playing to rehearse alternative responses and become comfortable using them.

Teaching students how to problem solve is another way of improving their ability to apply information. Put students in real life or simulated situations that are difficult or challenging, and show them how to develop and evaluate solutions based on available information. Such activities can be used to teach a wide variety of behavioral applications including play techniques, risk taking, study strategies and social interactions. For example, use existing social situations, or have students role play them, to teach how to use context cues to choose proper greetings, discussion topics or conversational approaches. Or use a similar approach to show them how to deal with stressful situations such as getting in trouble with a teacher, having an argument with a friend or responding to a playground bully. In each case, you create or choose circumstances to help students apply information in the setting to develop an effective behavioral response.

Knowing how to make judgments about behavior is an important area of self-discipline because it helps students align their performance with behavioral demands and circumstances. Managing judgments enables students to regulate and adjust their own behavior rather than having to rely on others for direction, guidance and corrective feedback. As you teach students how to attend to, interpret, and apply information in the setting, they will become more confident and successful in judging their performance.

Suggestions for Using Worksheet 5

Use **Worksheet 5** to develop a checklist to observe how well your students manage judgments about their performance. Some suggestions for using the worksheet are:

List judgments that involve specific determinations about performance

The items you describe should pertain to decisions about what to do (content), where to do it (location), how to do it (pacing), how much to do (quantity) and how well to do it (quality).

Limit your list to the most important judgments

Students typically make a wide array of determinations about their behavior, but not all of them will pertain to the issues you are concerned with. Focus your observations on decisions most important to helping students manage judgments in behavior areas you're concerned with.

List judgments for the entire performance sequence

It's usually easy to observe judgments during performance, but those that occur while students prepare for an activity and those taking place after they complete it can be just as crucial to successful performance.

Focus on judgments for positive behavior

Center your attention on judgments about being successful rather than unsuccessful because it will help you select skills that improve students' ability to manage judgments.

Set objectives that help students align behavior with performance conditions

These would be judgments that help students prepare for a task or activity, regulate and adjust their actions, evaluate progress, and improve when the next performance opportunity arises.

Worksheet 5 Example

Almost everyday after lunch, Mrs. Kelly's seventh graders come to class bickering or complaining about something a classmate did in the cafeteria. Billy and Jake got into another argument, Wally told everyone about Hanna's secret boyfriend, Lucy and Maria are not speaking to each other, Lance got in trouble again for swearing: The reports seem endless. In the past, Mrs. Kelly usually expressed proper concern over the incidence, admonished her students to behave, and discounted it as typical teenage rivalry. Now, she's not so sure that she has been using the best approach. The reports seem to be getting more frequent and other teachers are starting to voice their concern about her students' behavior.

Mrs. Kelly decided to begin eating lunch at the teacher's table in the cafeteria and take a first hand look at how her students behave. She saw right away that several had difficulty holding a proper conversation. They frequently interrupted, weren't thoughtful about things they said, misjudged each others' comments and body language and displayed many other problems. She decided that some difficulties come from students not judging what to say and when to say it and misreading social cues. Mrs. Kelly decided to address these problems more directly in her teaching.

She began her investigation by carefully watching how successful students hold their conversations. During lunchtime, she sat close enough to the student tables to overhear discussions, and she found other opportunities to listen unobtrusively to student groups. From these observations, she developed a list of judgments that competent students made during conversations and watched how they adjusted their behavior. She was surprised to see how well the students monitored and evaluated cues other group members gave about such things as their interest in topics, the proper language and tone to use, attitudes on touchy issues and the mood and feelings they displayed. She also noted how they frequently modified speech patterns and gestures to conform to group expectations. She described judgments she saw on a worksheet, and used them to observe some of her students, focusing mostly on ones who had the most difficulty with their interactions. Over several days, she rated how students did on each of the judgments on her list. She noticed that they often lost the thread of a conversation because they misjudged how much attention to give to the group. Sometimes, they seemed to think they could maintain two conversations at the same time, one with their friends and another with a group across the table. It was also apparent that they had difficulty gauging the impact of their comments, hurting a friend's feelings or causing an unintended argument.

She described her most pressing concerns with these objectives:

— learn to judge whether they are listening closely enough to follow the flow of the conversation,

— learn to judge whether it is the appropriate time to make a comment,

— learn to judge whether to continue talking on a topic or to change to a new topic,

— learn to judge whether their comments and body language are showing the proper support or sensitivity to another person's feelings.

Mrs. Kelly sees now that she misjudged the difficulties students were having. She realizes the importance of addressing these areas in her teaching so students do better at regulating and adjusting their behavior during peer conversations.

Worksheet 5: Observing judgements and setting objectives for instruction.

Name: _Mrs. Kelly_ Date: _November 1_

Student or group: _Lunch groups_ Grade: _7_

Task or Activity to be the Focus of Instruction: Conversations during lunch time

Judgments Pertaining to the Activity:	1st	2nd	3rd	4th	5th	Comments
Judgements about content:						
Whether they are listening to what others are saying	O	+	O	O	O	
Whether they know enough about the topic to discuss it	O	+	+	+	+	
Whether they are reacting properly to what others are saying	+	O	+	+	O	
Whether they are using the right language and gestures	O	+	O	O	O	
Judgments about pacing:						
Whether they are thinking through what they say before responding	+	O	+	O	O	
Whether it is the appropriate time to make a comment	O	+	O	O	O	
Whether they are answering the questions others ask of them	+	+	+	+	+	
Whether they should continue talking on a topic or change to a new one	O	+	O	O	O	
Judgments about quality:						
Whether they are communicating their feelings and opinions accurately	O	O	O	+	O	
Whether they are speaking clearly enough	+	+	+	+	+	
Whether their comments and gestures are showing the proper support and sensitivity	O	O	O	+	O	
Judgments about quantity:						
Whether they are talking too much, or too little	O	+	O	O	+	
Whether they are staying on a particular topic for too long a time span	O	+	+	+	O	
Whether they are focusing enough attention on the people in their group	+	O	O	+	O	
Judgments about placement of performance:						
Whether they are watching the people who're responding to their comments	+	+	+	O	O	
Whether they're focusing their attention	O	O	O	+	+	
Whether their comments and body language are showing the proper support or sensitivity to another person's feelings	O	O	+	O	O	

Judgements Observed (+ = makes correctly, 0 = does not make effectively)

Worksheet 5: Observing judgements and setting objectives for instruction.

Name: _____ Date: _____

Student or group: _____ Grade: _____

Task or Activity to be the Focus of Instruction:						
Judgements Pertaining to the Activity:	**Judgements Observed (+ = makes correctly 0 = does not make effectively):**					
	1st	2nd	3rd	4th	5th	Comments

Chapter 6

Planning and Monitoring Teaching Lessons

The Planning Process

Most teachers have a favorite format for writing lesson plans. It might be an approach learned in a college methods course, an idea borrowed from a colleague, a standardized form required by the school, or a published resource. Any of these sources can provide a useful and versatile system for laying out plans for teaching self-discipline. But more important than the way you write out your plans is the approach you take to planning itself. The methods you use to teach self-discipline will be most effective when you direct them toward meeting the instructional needs of students you are working with. The first section of the chapter describes a process for preparing teaching lessons no matter what format you use to document your plans. The second part explains how to monitor and evaluate your lessons so you can track student progress in learning the self-discipline skills you are teaching.

Elaborating and Expanding on Key Ideas

In the last three chapters we discussed a wide variety of methods for teaching self-discipline skills. Almost all teachers begin the planning process with a number of rough ideas like these for addressing their objectives. The best way to turn ideas into fully developed plans is to look at them critically and select the best ones to build on. Start your planning with just two or three key teaching ideas, and these should be ones that involve students and capture their interest, while representing a departure from things you have tried in the past. By choosing just a few of your best ideas as the centerpiece of your lesson, you avoid the logistical headaches that result from addressing several areas of instruction at once.

After you identify methods to build on, move toward more concrete planning by thinking through the details of putting these initiatives into action:

— when and where will you carry out the activities?

— what types of interactions will you and the students engage in during this time?

— what materials or equipment will you need?

— how will the group be structured?

— will the students work individually or in groups?

— how will activities be integrated with your other teaching?

As you think through the specifics of putting your ideas into practice, your procedures will become more organized and concrete.

You should also consider how to enlarge or expand on the procedures. Include practice opportunities for students to rehearse and refine new skills. Consider how to adapt the approaches to address other instructional objectives at the same time. Think of other settings in which to extend your procedures, or colleagues or other students you would like to bring in. You might wish to combine an approach with other teaching ideas. By combining and adding other elements like these, you develop a comprehensive lesson plan without losing sight of the central ideas that anchor your instruction. This approach of working out the fine points and expanding the scope of just a few key procedures will help ensure the focus and unity of your plans while allowing for creative exploration and rigorous attention to detail. The following are some guidelines to keep in mind.

Keep Procedures Simple, Dynamic and Flexible

Making procedures detailed and wide-ranging doesn't mean making them complex or elaborate. In fact, the most powerful instructional approaches are often very simple: Teaching students the basic steps for asking questions, highlighting benefits of getting along with playmates, showing them how to use work samples to check answers and correct errors, and using role plays to demonstrate and practice ways to handle disagreements. The planning process shouldn't make procedures more complicated; it should focus on getting the most out of them through thoughtful implementation. Procedures that are too elaborate, that involve too many new concepts, that require too many steps, or that ask for too high a level of understanding are likely to lose their focus and leave students confused.

At the same time, procedures will be more effective if they represent a change from the usual routine. Activities that simply repeat what has been done in the past or make only slight variations from existing conditions usually have little effect on student behavior. On the other hand, you can give instruction a surprising amount of impact simply by introducing change. Teach a lesson in a different location, for example, or have students lead an activity themselves. Change grouping arrangements, use new materials, or begin a lesson by giving a student a leadership role she isn't accustomed to. By doing something unusual or dynamic, you capture student attention and interest and give your lessons a greater chance at success.

Bear in mind that you can't anticipate all potential effects or complications that may arise. Plan procedures so you can adjust them if students are not responding as you expected or if conditions change in ways you didn't foresee. Lesson plans that are too rigid can put you in the difficult position of having to either continue activities that clearly are not working or scrapping your plans entirely. You can keep your teaching closely aligned with student needs by giving yourself leeway in your planning to shift or adapt procedures as needed.

Plan Collaboratively

Preparing teaching lessons provides a good opportunity to work with colleagues. This can be especially important in schools that do not have a strong atmosphere of teamwork or shared responsibility. Instructional planning often breaks down barriers with even the most isolated and resistant colleagues because it allows you to approach them with a request for advice rather than with suggestions or critiques. Collaboration usually makes lessons richer and more extensive because it adds new ideas and perspectives and helps overcome your own limitations and biases. It also helps establish the groundwork for teaching more collaboratively as well. Since other teachers often have a vested interest in the outcomes of your lessons, offer them the possibility of using successful activities in their settings as well. When you collaborate with teachers at your same grade level or across special and general education settings, you can build a unified approach for promoting self-discipline in students during the entire school day.

> **"Teachers are usually taught to think in terms of the different things they do for students; consequently instructional approaches they devise, even when innovative and dynamic, are often teacher — centered."**

Take a Student — Centered Approach

Teachers often overlook the opportunities and benefits of involving students as active participants in their own learning. Teachers are usually taught to think in terms of the different things they do for students; consequently instructional approaches they devise, even when innovative and dynamic, are often teacher — centered. The teacher presents the instructional content, directs the activity, gives the feedback and evaluates the results. Such approaches cast students as passive recipients of instruction rather than as active learners, and often work against the very self-discipline skills we want them to develop and use.

Students can participate in all the stages of planning and implementing lessons. You can involve them in the planning by surveying their interests, discussing your objectives, and including them in the preparation of materials and activities. During the lesson, have them give the directions, model skilled behavior, help one another practice new skills and take charge of prompting. Give students a role in measuring their progress and evaluating the lesson. Of course, the particular tasks and responsibilities you give them will depend on their age and abilities, but even those in the earliest grades or with significant disabilities can share in planning and conducting lessons. Student involvement creates a high level of excitement in learners, and makes learning less dependent on the charisma and expertise of the teacher. A student-centered approach allows you to become the facilitator for student learning rather than being the main focus of learning.

Writing the Lesson Plan

Lesson plans need to be written in a formal and complete manner. Those that are sketchy or vague cause activities to lose focus, shift away from the original objectives and cause you to overlook important elements that you should consider before you begin. By contrast, detailed plans allow you to anticipate factors in implementing the procedures, and give you a reference point during the lessons that helps keep activities centered on your objectives.

The primary consideration in deciding what information to include in a plan is whether that information will be useful in thinking through and in carrying out activities you have planned. Instructional plans should contain the following elements:

Basic information

Your name, the date, the student or group you will be working with and the setting where instruction will take place. This type of information will help your lessons serve as a future record of what you have done.

Instructional Objectives

They provide a referent for reviewing your plans and for carrying out the activities so you can adjust procedures to ensure that the lesson remains focused on your goals.

Procedures

This detailed description of teaching methods allows you to consider the requirements of your lessons and avoid making unintended changes during your teaching. You can sometimes cut corners with this, however. For instance, if you make a worksheet or outline for students to use, attach it to the plan and make a note about where it fits in the overall activity.

Materials/Personnel

Don't forget to list equipment and materials that must be obtained or set up in advance, or personnel who will assist with the activities. Including these items in the plan will help you remember to make the necessary arrangements ahead of time.

Schedule

This outlines the procedures you will be using each day, and helps you decide how to integrate your teaching within the normal classroom or school routine. When you write the schedule, think about what else will be going on before, during and after the activities, and consider ways to take advantage of or work around the normal routine.

Monitoring

This describes how you will document the results of your teaching. Monitoring is a crucial area because it can tell you if your lesson is meeting its objectives and what kinds of initiatives might be needed next. Monitoring is so important that we will cover it at length in the next section.

Follow-up

This describes what you plan to do after instruction is finished. You should think ahead to your follow-up on a lesson, because it can be an important stepping-stone to further work with the students regardless of whether the results are positive.

Writing a Narrative

In addition to writing out the basic elements of a lesson, it's helpful to prepare a narrative or script that gives a day-by-day account of what you and the students will be doing and of what you hope to accomplish. Writing out plans permits a careful consideration of factors you must address in carrying out the procedures. It amounts to a written rehearsal – going through each element of the lesson and indicating exactly what must be done to make each part of the plan flow smoothly. Teachers have frequently reported that writing a narrative helps them consider potential problems before they arise and to think through their teaching in greater detail than they normally would. At the end of the chapter, there is a planning worksheet that includes a portion of a lesson narrative. As you can see in **Worksheet 6a**, the tone of the narrative is informal but the information is specific enough to allow you to think through the details for implementing lesson.

The Monitoring Process

When you have completed your planning, you will want to begin teaching. But before you start, there is one question you must consider: How you will monitor results of your instruction? If you begin the lesson without a clear monitoring plan, you will miss essential information you should be watching for, have difficulty interpreting the results you see and be unsure how to proceed with the next activities. Accordingly, you should take a few minutes more before you begin to sketch out a plan for monitoring the lesson.

Monitoring is the process of observing and recording the effects of instruction on student behavior. It involves highly formalized tests, charts, graphs, and recording forms, but it can also involve simple tally marks and informal notes. The function of these procedures is to indicate/demonstrate how well a lesson meets its stated objectives. Teachers often neglect to consider monitoring when they plan instruction because they feel that they have enough to do with getting lessons underway, or that it's more complicated or time-consuming than it's worth. Or they may think they will be able to tell how instruction is going as a matter of course, and do not need to plan special procedures to record the obvious. But such beliefs are often not borne out in reality. When lessons have unexpected or disappointing results, teachers are often puzzled and dismayed. They can't account for the results they see and have difficulty knowing how to revise or reconfigure their plans. They may in frustration end up attributing the difficulties to "unteachable" students who "refuse to learn."

Carefully planned monitoring can alleviate such problems because it does more than document obvious results. Monitoring assists in identifying and responding to changes in student behavior, in keeping instruction focused, in helping you watch for subtle effects that might pass unnoticed, and in providing a referent for deciding how to proceed once your original instruction has been completed. When lessons have disappointing results, monitoring can help you spot the sources of difficulty and revise or redirect instruction. Monitoring makes lessons not so much a one-time quick fix as an ongoing process, one in which the initial instructional plan is only a starting point for a responsive, flexible approach to teaching self-discipline.

"Monitoring assists in identifying and responding to changes in student behavior, in keeping instruction focused, in helping you watch for subtle effects that might pass unnoticed, and in providing a referent for deciding how to proceed once your original instruction has been completed."

Principles of Effective Monitoring

Whether you are teaching a group of students or an individual, your approach to monitoring will direct your attention to the major questions you have about student behavior and the essential elements of your lessons. It should help you assess key behaviors you are concerned with and allow you to make informed decisions about follow-up instruction. Monitoring can assist in the following ways:

Monitoring focuses attention on key issues

In the middle of a lesson, it's difficult to decide what you should be paying attention to: Is it the number of times students are participating in an activity or the accuracy of the responses they give? The amount of attention they pay the teacher? The language they use? How they handle feedback or criticism? By planning what to look for in advance, you direct attention toward the areas of behavior that really concern you and screen out the rest.

Monitoring helps determine whether instruction is on track

Conditions can shift rapidly during a lesson and it's easier than you think to unknowingly adjust procedures and change the emphasis of your teaching. A lesson in how to ask questions about assignment directions can quickly become a lesson on remedial academic skills if you loose sight of your aims. If you wait until after the original plans are complete to consider how things went, it's too late to make changes or redirect activities to keep them on track. On the other hand, when you plan monitoring as an integral part of instruction, Evaluate whether the procedures are in line with your objectives and make adjustments as needed.

Monitoring gauges effects of instructional procedures

Often lessons and interventions have effects that are quite different from those you anticipate. For example, students can become so engrossed in an instructional game or skit that they miss out in learning the skills activities were supposed to teach. By monitoring student responses on a daily basis, you address such effects quickly and refocus lessons on the behavior you want students to learn.

Monitoring judges if instruction is meeting its aims

The most basic judgment you need to make about lessons is whether they are helping to improve student behavior. If your aim is to teach students to ask questions when they need help, for instance, you need to be able to judge whether their question asking has become proficient. If you want them to use encouraging language during peer interactions, be prepared to observe their speech patterns once the lessons have taken place. Without monitoring, making such determinations about the effects of instruction is largely a matter of guesswork and intuition.

Monitoring is not just about recording results in a particular way; rather, it's about directing your attention to the behaviors and issues that are most important for making decisions about continuing, extending and revising instruction.

Monitoring and Standards

You should begin the monitoring process by deciding on the particular issues you wish to assess. The most important element in monitoring is the standards you use to gauge student competence. Standards indicate the minimal level of behavior students must reach to perform a task or activity successfully. Each standard designates a specific number or level that represents acceptable or "C-level" behavior. This level allows you to make clear determinations during and after instruction about whether students are making progress in the task or activity you are teaching, and whether you should continue or revise your lesson.

For most classroom applications, you set standards for lessons by asking two basic questions:

1. What behavior should I count to determine whether students are improving in the task or activity?

2. What level do they need to reach to show minimal (or "C-level") competence?

The first question focuses on what to look for in order to assess student progress on the particular task you are teaching. This might be the number of times students add comments to a discussion, the number of minutes they take to complete a worksheet, the number of problems they answer correctly, or the number of times they argue during recess. The second question identifies the target level that marks minimally competent performance. This could be at least two comments per discussion, no more than ten minutes per assignment, at least 70% of problems assigned, or no more than one time a week.

The first stage in teaching students to manage the self-discipline dimensions of performance, motivation, and judgments (Chapters 3-5) is to decide on a task or activity that will be the focus of instruction. Examples of such tasks are "Working on assignments in study groups," "Playing group games during recess" and "Studying spelling words for a weekly quiz." With most tasks there is a natural way to evaluate student behavior. In the three examples above, count the number of assignments students complete, the number of minutes they play cooperatively in groups and the number of words they spell correctly on a quiz. Thus, you define standards by describing the most natural or direct way of keeping track of student behavior. Sometimes it will be easier and more natural to observe instances of incompetent or unsuccessful behavior. For example, count the number of times students do not complete assignments, the amount of time they are out of their seats or number of times they don't follow teacher direction. If you follow the most straightforward and typical way of counting behavior, your standards will be easy to use in classroom applications.

In addition, standards define a specific number that represents minimally competent performance. If you are counting a positive, compliant behavior,

"Begin the monitoring process by deciding on the particular issues you wish to assess. The most important element in monitoring is the standards you use to gauge student competence. Standards indicate the minimal level of behavior students must reach to perform a task or activity successfully."

express the standard as "at least X times." For instance, to follow the examples in the paragraph above, the standards might be "at least one per class period (assignments completed), "at least 15 minutes per recess" (minutes playing cooperatively in groups), or "at least 70% percent correct" (spelling words on a quiz). If you are counting incompetent or unsuccessful performance, express the standard as "no more than X times." Again, using the examples above, the standards might be "no more than one per week" (times not completing assignments), "no more than two minutes per class" (number of times out of seat), or "no times" (number of times not following teacher direction). When the behavior is competent only in moderation, designate a number "between X and Y times." For example, state that students should add comments to discussions at least one time per class but not more than five, or they can seem too outspoken or overbearing. In this case, specify the standard as "between one and five times." Table 6 gives more examples of standards for tasks and activities.

When preparing lessons for individual students, standards should describe the minimum competent or average level of behavior for students in general education settings. This means you identify a somewhat lower or less demanding standard for individual than group lessons. When you teach single students, you are trying to raise their behavior to the average level of their peers; whereas, when you work with many students at once, you are trying to raise the average level of behavior for the entire group. In either case, the number you designate should not be an ideal or an expression of your own wishes; it should be an estimate based on your knowledge and observations of actual student behavior.

Use **Worksheet 6b** at the end of the chapter to guide your plans for monitoring. There are spaces for describing the standards for the task or activity you are teaching and this is where you identify the particular behavior you will count and indicate what numbers the students should perform at least, no more than or between.

Other Issues to Monitor

In addition there are other important issues you will want to assess during teaching. They include questions about the procedures you are using, the skills you are teaching, and broader questions about the student self-discipline and independence. There is usually so much going on during a lesson that it's a good idea before beginning instruction to spend a few minutes brainstorming key questions to monitor. Attach your questions to **Worksheets 6a** and **b** to provide a more comprehensive monitoring plan.

Five Monitoring Issues

1. How are Students Performing in the Overall Task or Activity?

Although individual objectives give a clear indication of student progress, it's important not to lose sight of the primary aim of the lesson, which is to teach students how to become more self-disciplined. Keeping a broad perspective on the original task or activity you selected helps you see the full implications of student learning and decide what areas to emphasize next. Some questions you might ask are:

— Is student performance more accurate or competent for the circumstances they are in? Does their behavior still stand out from the group norm?

— Are they more self-reliant in completing assignments or participating in activities? Do they take more initiative and responsibility for doing what's asked of them?

— Are they able to control or regulate their actions more effectively? Do they seem to be getting along better with teachers and classmates?

— Are classmates and teachers responding more favorably to student behavior?

2. What are Student Reactions to Instructional Procedures?

When you are using novel or dynamic approaches, watch carefully to be sure student reactions are positive and directed toward behaviors you're teaching. Examples of the kinds of questions you might list are:

— Do the role-playing situations improve student motivation to problem solve?

— Are they able to carry out the five-step procedure for judging their game playing? Do I need to simplify it?

— Do the learning center activities encourage students to work together more effectively? Do they increase or decrease on-task behavior?

— Are they able to follow the directions and use the materials I give them on their own?

3. How Do I Coordinate Instruction With Student Progress?

The procedures you use must be timed and coordinated to match student progress if they're to be effective. Students will need to understand a concept before they practice it, or need to master basic skills before they use them in real situations. In such cases, be ready to monitor their progress in the early parts of the lessons in order to coordinate procedures in the later parts of your plans. Examples of specific questions in this area include:

— Are students ready to try conversational patterns on their own?

— Have they learned to work together well enough to choose their own study groups?

— Is my teaching going slow enough for students to ask questions or formulate opinions about the topic?

— Are they able to judge their own work habits so I can reduce the teacher-directed feedback I give them?

4. How Well Do Students Carry Over or Adapt New Skills?

One of the most gratifying effects of instruction is when students carry over the behavior you are teaching to new settings and circumstances. It's even more rewarding when they begin developing skills in entirely new behavior areas following the momentum they have gained from the lessons. This expansion confirms important strides students are making, and suggests areas for future work in supporting and extending skills. Examples of questions that look at carryover include:

— Are students taking initiative in other situations besides this one?

— Is the target student joining peer groups at lunch or on the playground?

— Are students able to judge and evaluate their performance during large group discussions in other subject areas or classrooms?

— Is the student's improvement in assignments leading to more positive interactions with other teachers?

5. What New Information am I Learning About the Students?

Chapters 3-5 discussed the importance of observation and assessment in learning about the performance characteristics of individuals and groups. This investigation need not end when instruction begins. In fact, lessons are likely to provide you with new information about student abilities and inclinations, as you see their responses under new conditions and with new behaviors. Examples of questions you might list include:

— Are students able to adapt to different teaching approaches and activities?

— Does their motivation maintain over time or does helping students generate motivation need to be an ongoing consideration in teaching?

— How well do they attend to multiple cues in judging informal interactions with classmates? Are certain cues easier (or more difficult) for them to attend to?

— Can they integrate new study skills into their repertoire or does this need to be a focus of the next lesson?

"Because standards designate the specific areas you count in order to evaluate your lesson, they give a good indication of how to monitor student progress."

Approaches for Monitoring

The first thing to consider in planning monitoring procedures is the issues to watch for, and in particular, the standards for your lesson. Because standards designate the specific areas you count in order to evaluate your lesson, they give a good indication of how to monitor student progress. For instance, if a standard indicates that you count the number of times students complete assignments, you need a procedure to track the number of assignments they finish. Or if the standard involves the number of defiant comments they make, you need a procedure to monitor how often they make this type of comment. You can track such numbers by keeping notes or tallies. The trick is being in the right position to record them.

You will find approaches in Chapters 3-5 for observing student behavior that work equally well for monitoring the effects of lessons. Here are five methods for monitoring:

1. Direct observation is usually very reliable, as long as you conduct it in an unobtrusive manner and make sure teaching responsibilities do not interfere with tracking student behavior.

2. Using other observers to help with monitoring is a good option when you expect to be busy or want to record behavior across class periods or places. In such cases, be sure the other observers know precisely what behavior to track and when to make a tally.

3. Video can also be helpful, as it allows you to watch student behavior carefully and to make precise counts. When using video, set up the camera well in advance so the students acclimate to it and make sure you're aware of what to include in the camera shot.

4. Self-monitoring forms or devices involve students in measuring their own behavior. Not only does this give them an active role in their instruction, it helps make monitoring a more integral and natural part of the learning process.

5. Follow-up interviews or conversations with students taking part in the lessons can be used to gain a different point of view on what you see and helps clarify behavior that was unclear or ambiguous.

Making a Daily Log

Spend a few minutes when instructional activities are finished to record observations and make comments. If you wait until the end of the school day or later, you're likely to forget or gloss over important details. Furthermore, making timely entries in a log gives you an opportunity to take stock of how the activities are going and to plan adjustments as needed. You will see results that surprise you or that suggest other directions for instruction, so don't treat lesson plans as set in stone. As long as you approach instruction in a planned and consistent manner and keep a focus on the objectives you defined, you can be flexible and responsive to ongoing results. The worksheet at the end of the chapter shows spaces for a daily log of tallies and comments.

Following up on Lessons

Once you've finished your lesson, it's easy to relax and view the task as finished. But it is important to take stock of your results and reflect on skills students have learned and those they will learn next. Teaching is an ongoing process and whether results are positive or negative, they serve as a springboard for planning the next stage of instruction. When your lessons didn't produce results you had hoped for, review your plan to see where changes may be necessary. Sometimes all that is needed is to continue the lesson a little longer to allow more time for learning to take place. In other instances, you need to make more substantial changes, such as the following:

— revising objectives so they are more in line with student needs,

— developing new teaching procedures or changing those that are clearly not effective,

— addressing student incentive needs more directly,

— reducing competing behaviors that distract or misdirect learning.

When the results of your lessons are positive, follow-up by selecting another task for students to apply new skills or by working with other school personnel to extend their progress school wide. You may also wish to teach students how to advance self-discipline skills further. The next chapters discuss two areas to concentrate on: Managing habits (Chapter 7) and managing school and personal goals (Chapter 8).

Suggestions for Using Worksheet 6a

You can easily adapt Worksheet 6a to planning lessons for groups or individuals. Here are six suggestions for using this form:

1. Adapt the worksheet to your needs

You may already be using forms to prepare teaching lessons. This worksheet is not designed to replace them but to highlight key elements of the planning process and supplement your forms where necessary. For example, your forms may not include a space for a narrative describing the procedures but this description can prove an extremely useful tool.

2. List Objectives Prominently in Your Plans

The worksheet gives a prominent place for listing instructional objectives. These represent the thrust of your lessons, so it's important to put them up front to keep your focus clear while planning and carrying out the activities.

3. Include a Listing of Equipment, Materials and Personnel

Providing spaces on your worksheet to list materials you need to prepare and resources you plan to use will ensure that everything is ready when you begin teaching.

> **"When the results of your lessons are positive, follow-up by selecting another task for students to apply new skills or by working with other school personnel to extend their progress school wide."**

4. Consider Drafting a Narrative of Instructional Plans

Although this might seem like unnecessary paperwork, a narrative gives you a chance to go over plans in careful detail, providing a mental rehearsal. Describing activities on a day-by-day basis will help you consider logistical aspects of the lesson such as the sequence and coordination of various procedures and possible reactions of the students. A narrative need not be formal or seamless, but should indicate what you do each day to think the activities through.

5. Plan in advance materials and personnel you need

This is a simple step, but many lesson formats overlook these details. Making a list of the equipment you will need and the colleagues who will take part can help you remember to make these arrangements before you begin.

6. Make out a simple schedule

A schedule of activities is a useful way to summarize your overall plans. Here you can outline the various approaches or activities you will use each day so you can review how the lesson fits together.

Suggestions for Using Worksheet 6b

This worksheet is designed to simplify the process of identifying standards and help you monitor effects of instruction on student behavior. Suggestions for using the worksheet:

1. Take the time to identify standards

Standards are an important component of the teaching process because they provide the benchmark for determining overall effectiveness of your instruction. The approach presented here is designed to make it simple to quickly identify a clear standard for evaluating student progress in each of the objectives you have set for instruction.

2. Consider the most natural way to count a particular behavior

Teachers usually keep an informal mental account of student behavior. Identifying standards is a matter of expressing elements you implicitly keep track of anyway, like the number of times students interrupt during discussion, the number of minutes they remain on task or the number of arguments they get in during recess.

3. Choose whether standards designate minimum or maximum behavior

In most cases you can describe standards as "at least" or "no more than" a certain number. These terms indicate whether the standard indicates a minimum amount of positive or a maximum amount of contrary behavior. Indicate a range "between X and Y" to show that a behavior has minimum and maximum limits.

4. Standards should be realistic

The numbers you designate in standards should not represent your wishes, or even requirements. Instead, they should indicate minimum "C-level" behavior representing the dividing line between competent and incompetent performance.

5. Describe other issues you want to address

Although it's important to keep a focus on objectives you have set for instruction, there are other issues you will keep track of as well. Take a couple minutes to think about other factors you need to monitor as the lesson progresses.

6. Keep a daily tally of results

Tallying students behavior as it occurs and summarizing results at the end of each day are the best ways to describe subtle results you see on your instructional plans. Once your plans are complete, these daily results will make a good basis for deciding how to follow up on activities

Worksheet Example 6

Ms. Mitchell, a special education teacher at Northside High School, is concerned that some students on her caseload in general education settings aren't participating well in classroom activities and lack initiative in doing their work and interacting with classmates. She discussed these problems with Mr. Thompson, who has four of her students in his tenth grade English class and he confirmed her observations. He also noted that two general education students

"Teaching is an ongoing process and whether results are positive or negative, they serve as a springboard for planning the next stage of instruction."

in this class have the same difficulties. These six students are usually well behaved, but show little self-direction in work habits and require a lot of one-on-one direction, encouragement and feedback. Mr. Thompson says that when he's not able to watch closely over them, they are at a loss how to proceed with activities. Usually they stop working and wait until he can get to them.

After observing these students' behavior more closely, Ms. Mitchell and Mr. Thompson have come up with objectives that focus on teaching them how to take more initiative in classroom activities and to show self-direction in completing assignments. The overall aim is to teach them to use their self-selected classmates as models of good work habits and rely on them for guidance, direction and support. The aim also includes teaching them to make judgments about their work habits based on classmate performance to evaluate their own progress on assigned tasks and learn to take more pride and satisfaction in doing assignments without teacher intervention.

Once teachers formulated their ideas, they prepared a lesson plan to help guide implementation of the procedures. **Worksheet 6a** shows the first page of this plan. They began by listing overall lesson objectives to keep them foremost in their minds. Then they wrote a narrative on what to do each day in the lesson. The teachers found this process helped them consider details of timing and logistics they would've overlooked otherwise. Finally, they made a list of materials and personnel to be involved, and prepared a schedule they referred to as the lesson progressed. After Ms. Mitchell and Mr. Thompson finalized the plan, they felt they were prepared to direct a positive and productive lesson plan for these students.

The teachers realize that they will need to monitor these student behaviors closely as they carry out their teaching. Their more informal attempts to help these students have not been effective in the past and this time they want to be able to react quickly and accurately to the responses these students show. The teachers begin by identifying standards for each of their objectives. **Worksheet 6b** shows how they described them. On subsequent pages, they listed other issues they want to assess, such as how target students react to using classmate models; whether they become too dependent on them for direction and support; and whether they take sufficient pride in tasks they accomplish without teacher encouragement. The teachers described their monitoring procedures, which included having target students keep a record of tasks they complete with (and without) teacher intervention.

The teachers are now ready to start the lesson. Every day, Mr. Thompson will evaluate each student's work and record the number of times he has to give individualized direction and support to keep them working. Ms. Mitchell will keep a daily log of other observations and results and prepare a summary of their findings. They will confer at the end of the school day to review progress on the lesson and discuss modifications in day-to-day activities.

Table 6: Examples of standards for tasks and activities

Task/Activity	What to Count	Level of Minimum Competence
Completes assignments	Number of worksheet questions answered correctly	At least 8 of 10 worksheet questions
Expresses interests and desires to teacher	Number of times expresses interests/desires	At least two times per period
Talks with peers without arguing	Number of times argues	Less than 1 per lunch period
Works in study groups	Number of minutes works with group	At least 10 minutes per group activity
Gives comments during class discussions	Number of comments	Between 1 and 5 comments per discussion
Plays games during recess	Number of minutes	At least 10 minutes per recess
Engages in playful teasing	Number of times classmates complain about teasing	No more than 1 time per period

Worksheet 6a: Preparing teaching lessons

Name: _Ms. Mitchell/Mr. Thompson_ Date: _November 1_

Student or group: _Self-direction Group_ Grade: _11_

Task or Activity to be the Focus of Instruction: _Independent work time_

Lesson/Intervention Objectives:

Learn to _complete assignments without teacher oversight_

Learn to _judge how to continue with a task to its completion_

Learn to _use a classmate for direction and support_

Learn to _take pride in doing tasks without teacher intervention_

Learn to

Narrative of Lesson/Intervention Plans:

On the first day of the lesson during study period, Mr. Thompson will meet with the "Self-direction Group" to discuss what good work habits are and to ask the students to identify classmates in English who they feel show good work habits. He will have each of them choose one classmate as a mentor to sit by and get help from while doing in-class assignments. Mr. Thompson will explain that he wants them to do more of their work without asking him for help and their mentors will be able to give them support if they need it. He will then give them a self-recording logbook and ask them to complete a page each English period. On a page are spaces for entering the day's assignment and recording how much of it they completed and the grade, and for tallying the number of times they ask or wait for the teacher's assistance. Later in the study period, Mr. Thompson will meet with the classmates the group members selected, ask them whether they would like to help the target students with their work, and outline guidelines for offering assistance, such as showing them how to do the work rather than doing it for them., and giving recognition for work that is done independently.

On the second day, Mr. Thompson will begin English class by setting a new seating arrangement that has each of the Self-direction Group sit by his/her self-selected mentor. Ms. Mitchell will be team teaching with Mr. Thompson this day and she will oversee the mentor-mentee pairs to clarify the teachers' expectations and offer ideas for giving assistance and support. After class or in study hall, Mr. Thompson will talk to each pair and find out. . .

Worksheet 6b: Monitoring teaching lessons.

Name: ___Ms. Mitchell/Mr. Thompson_____ Date: _November 1_

Student or group: _____Self-direction group_____ Grade: __11___

Task or Activity to be the Focus of Instruction: _Independent work time_

Monitoring Lesson/Intervention Objectives:

Objective: Learn to ___complete assignments without teacher oversight___

What to measure or count to judge this objective:

Number of ___assignments completed and their grades___

Standard for this objective (defining average or "c-level" behavior):

[X] At least ___4 with "C"s___ per ___week___

[ ] No more than _____ per _____

[ ] Between _____ and _____ per _____

Objective: Learn to ___judge how to continue with a task to its completion___

What to measure or count to judge this objective:

Number of ___times asks teachers or mentor for direction___

Standard for this objective (defining average or "c-level" behavior):

[ ] At least _____ per _____

[X] No more than ___2___ per ___assignment___

[ ] Between _____ and _____ per _____

Worksheet 6a: Preparing teaching lessons

Name: _____ Date: _____

Student or group: _____ Grade: _____

Task or Activity to be the Focus of Instruction:

Lesson/Intervention Objectives:

Learn to

Learn to

Learn to

Learn to

Learn to

Narrative of Lesson/Intervention Plans:

Worksheet 6b: Monitoring teaching lessons.

Name: _____ Date: _____

Student or group: _____ Grade: _____

Task or Activity to be the Focus of Instruction:

Monitoring Lesson/Intervention Objectives:

Objective: Learn to _____

What to measure or count to judge this objective:

Number of _____

Standard for this objective (defining average or "c-level" behavior):

☐   At least _____ per _____

☐   No more than _____ per _____

☐   Between _____ and _____ per _____

Objective: Learn to _____

What to measure or count to judge this objective:

Number of _____

Standard for this objective (defining average or "c-level" behavior):

☐   At least _____ per _____

☐   No more than _____ per _____

☐   Between _____ and _____ per _____

Chapter 7

Managing Habits

Extending the Teaching of Self-Discipline Skills

So far in the book we have been discussing how to teach students to manage performance, motivation and judgments. Learning to use these fundamental self-discipline skills in everyday school situations will help students attain greater competence and independence in their behaviors. In the next two chapters, we will look at ways to show students how to combine and extend these basic skills to achieve even greater levels of self-discipline. This chapter focuses on teaching the skills for managing habits. **Habits** are the building blocks of efficient, productive behavior, because they help students develop fluency and consistency in their performance and make it easier for them to do routine tasks and activities.

Habits and Self-Discipline

A habit is a consistent patterned way of carrying out a series of performance steps. We develop habits by repeatedly linking together a series of steps until it becomes a single unit of behavior that we use to complete a task or activity. Once we have formed a habit, our actions become automatic: We carry out the steps without deliberately thinking about them or the conditions around us. We manage habits by building consistent behavior patterns that meet the demands of routine activities and integrating these habits in an overall performance sequence. Our ability to manage habits aids us in carrying out a wide variety of everyday tasks from getting dressed in the morning, fixing breakfast and preparing for work; to teaching our students at school, talking with colleagues and grading assignments; to brushing our teeth and preparing for bed at night. When you drove to work this morning, you managed many habits. You got out your keys, put them in the ignition, started the motor and shifted into drive all as a single pattern of behavior or habit rather than as discrete deliberate actions. You followed your usual travel route to school managing various habits: Making adjustments in steering and driving speed, stopping for traffic signals, switching driving lanes and parking in the teacher's lot all without giving each action involved a second thought. Your facility in knowing how and when to use habits like these help you with getting to school each day, and make the routine and sometimes tedious task of driving there less demanding.

Students who are successful in their behavior also know how to manage habits that help them with everyday school tasks. These are simple things like saying "Good morning" to you as they enter the classroom, getting out textbooks when the bell rings, going to the same work tables at study time, and meeting friends on the way to lunch. They also manage habits to aid them with more complicated activities as well: Taking notes, studying for tests, completing assignments, holding conversations with teachers and classmates, and playing games during recess and gym. If you take the time to watch these students

> **"The ability to manage habits is an important aspect of self-discipline because it aids students with organizing and regulating their behavior and with being more self-directed and independent in the tasks they perform."**

carefully, you will see they follow the same organization in the notes they take, use the same strategies to review for tests, complete math problems using the same tricks and shortcuts, and talk with teachers and classmates using similar phrases and mannerisms. You will also notice variations in their behavior as they adapt to conditions, much like the way you adjust your driving when you encounter a slow vehicle or a pot hole in the road. Under normal circumstances, students use the same patterns of behavior in carrying out many routine tasks. Another important characteristic of this student behavior is that their habits are set in motion or "triggered" by environmental cues that signal when to use them. For example, entering your classroom and seeing you is a cue for their "Good morning" habit, the ring of the school bell triggers their "get out my books paper and pencil" habit, and telling them to begin study time signals their "leave my desk and go to my study table" habit.

The ability to manage habits like these is an important aspect of self-discipline because it aids students with organizing and regulating their behavior and with being more self-directed and independent in the tasks they do. A foremost attribute of a habit is that it improves student ability to meet the demands of the situation. Students develop and use a patterned way of taking notes, studying for tests, playing recess games and talking with teachers and classmates because these habits help them achieve success under routine conditions. And rather than having to work out each of the individual actions in an entire performance sequence, students use their habits to carry out many segments automatically, making it easier to manage their performance without outside support and direction. Habits also add to students' abilities to manage motivation and generate the incentive to carry out routine, repetitious and sometimes boring tasks. Because habits increase the overall fluency and ease of performance, they reduce the time and energy students need to complete these tasks. Habits help students achieve the outcomes of performance, and with less planning, energy and attention to details. Finally, habits help students with managing judgments because of the fewer decisions they have to make and the less need to focus on external cues for direction and feedback. Once they have developed a habit that suits a particular set of circumstances, they perform it as a single unit of behavior and rely on internal cues and feelings to guide much of their behavior. Successful students manage all kinds of habits in their everyday behavior and this ability increases their proficiency and confidence in doing routine tasks and activities.

Students who have difficulties with self-discipline may not have the proper habits to be successful in school or know how to manage them. While successful students use patterned, efficient methods for taking notes, completing assignments, playing with friends and many other things, the behavior of students with poorly formed habits is more deliberate, tentative or haphazard. Their actions lack the fluency and efficiency of competent students because without proper habits, they need to work out each individual action they perform and fit it in to an overall performance sequence. These students' study notes are poorly organized, their assignments not complete or correctly done, their play poorly timed and coordinated, and their interactions with teachers and classmates awkward and confused. Difficulties like these often arise when students fall behind the rest of the group as they try to figure out how to do things others do automatically. Invariably, these students have less motivation and self-confidence in doing routine tasks because it takes them more time, energy and effort to attain the same level of success as their proficient classmates. Moreover, as these students strive to overcome difficulties and search for ways to become successful, they develop habits that are inefficient and counter-productive.

Students' ability to manage habits thus plays an important function in furthering academic achievement and social competence, and aids teachers in fostering an orderly and well-structured classroom environment. All students, even your most competent ones, need to continually build new and more complex habits, and discover broader applications for the ones they already have, in order to progress further in school and be able to respond to more challenging situations.

Teaching Students to Manage Habits

You can teach students to manage habits by showing them how to combine the basic self-management skills of managing performance, motivation and judgments that we discussed in Chapters 3-5.

Managing habits involves:

— recognizing that some tasks are routine and repetitious and lend themselves to forming habits,

— developing generalized performance patterns that accomplish tasks under typical conditions,

— repeating the same series of actions until it becomes a patterned response or habit, i.e., until the behavior become fluent, efficient and self-directed,

— relying on internal cues to guide and direct use of habits,

— integrating habits in broader performance sequences,

— identifying situations and opportunities for using habits,

— adapting habits to changes in performance demands and circumstances and not using habits when conditions are unique,

— taking advantage of the outcomes and benefits of habits, e.g., using them as incentives to build even more efficient and effective habits.

You can use many of the procedures and worksheets presented in the previous chapters to choose the habits you would like students to manage and to prepare lesson plans to teach the needed skills. Begin by selecting a task or activity on which to focus your instruction. When teaching students to manage habits, the task or activity should be one they do on a routine and repetitive basis, and where their actions are fairly consistent for parts of the performance sequence. The key is to focus teaching on a task where forming a habit would add to the fluency, speed and efficiency of student behavior.

Students benefit from managing habits in the way they:

— prepare for the start of the class period,

— write their name and the date on the top of assignments,

— ask questions in a large group discussion,

— get out materials for homework review,

— do long division problems,

— give oral reports and group presentations,

— answer end of chapter questions,

— practice a musical instrument,

— review directions for daily assignments with study partners,

— pass in papers at the end of a class period.

> **"Students' ability to manage habits thus plays an important function in furthering academic achievement and social competence, and aids teachers in fostering an orderly and well-structured classroom environment."**

In informal situations, they benefit from managing habits in the way they:

— put their belongings away when they arrive at school,

— exchange greetings with adults they meet in the hallway,

— join up with friends on the way to lunch,

— line up for recess,

— throw, dribble or catch a ball, or run a variety of sports plays,

— go through the cafeteria line,

— use table manners during lunch or snack time,

— organize materials in school lockers or backpacks,

— assemble supplies and materials to take home after school,

— leave the school building to catch the bus.

When you work with individual students who have difficulty managing habits, it's helpful to look for habits successful students have and use them as instructional objectives for target students. This approach helps you direct your teaching on building patterns of behavior that produce the greatest improvements in the target students' performance.

In some situations only particular aspects of a task can be carried out as habits and you need to make this determination before you begin your teaching. For example, if you are teaching students to manage arithmetic computation habits when they do math assignments, first examine each problem and make a decision about which habit applies. In this case, only part of the task of "doing math assignments" would lend itself to forming habits. Preparing a list of performance steps, as discussed in Chapter 3, helps you identify the series of steps in a task that students can build into a habit. Such a list is useful with complicated tasks such as doing an oral report, participating in a large group discussion, taking study notes, or using a conflict resolution strategy. For example, sequencing performance steps for "preparing for the start of a class period" might show that the following segments would be well suited to forming a habit:

— goes to seat upon entering the classroom,

— puts books and supplies away,

— talks quietly with neighbor,

— sits down when teacher enters the room,

— stops talking and faces the teacher when the bell rings.

Developing a list of performance steps helps you decide whether to teach students to manage a task as a single unit or sub-divide it for separate lessons. Learning to manage individual segments apart from a larger task is beneficial when circumstances for instruction might be distracting or confusing to them. For example, students might find that managing a conflict resolution strategy is easier to learn as a separate pull-out lesson than as part of game playing, hallway conversations with peers, small group assignments or other situations where they would need to use the strategy. Isolating the conflict resolution component from other aspects of social interactions allows you to give it special emphasis so it more quickly becomes an established pattern in student behavior. You could teach the strategy as a separate lesson and have students practice it several times. Then, show them how to use their new habit, perhaps using skits or role playing, as part of ongoing activities and interactions.

After you select a task or task component to teach as a habit, begin planning instruction. The procedures you use should focus on showing students how to repeat performance steps the same way each time so they can develop a smooth, consistent pattern of behavior. A key consideration in your teaching is to highlight the importance of carrying out the steps correctly from the start of instruction, and not varying from the pattern that has been planned. Let's say, for example, that you are showing your students how to manage a habit in using a step-by-step approach for solving long division problems. Prepare your lessons so they learn to carry out the exact approach you are teaching and solve the first problem correctly. Then, have the students focus on repeating this same technique with the next division problem, the next one, and so on. In this way they quickly learn to form the habit without needing to unlearn any extra steps or mistakes they might add to the sequence when left to their own devices. It's worth taking extra time to ensure that students learn how to develop a patterned response even if you have to teach at a slower, more deliberate pace, subdivide the class into smaller groups, assign task partners, or instruct students individually.

Another factor to keep in mind is that the more closely spaced opportunities you can give students to practice a patterned response, the quicker and more established a habit becomes. As a general rule, have students practice a response until they can carry out the actions in a smooth, fluent, errorless pattern. In a task like doing long division, when you provide students with practice problems and if they continue using the step-by-step method you taught them to solve enough problems, they will learn to manage this approach on their own. Their solving of math problems becomes smoother, faster and more self-directed until they are doing long division without thinking about the steps they go through.

In some circumstances you may have to alter the students' normal schedule to provide sufficient practice opportunities, particularly when they have only a few chances each day to learn a patterned response. If you show students how to manage a habit for writing down assignments, a task that occurs once or twice a day, give them several extra practice opportunities in quick succession so they have enough time to develop and manage a patterned response. For example, sub-divide the day's homework into several mini-assignments to give them practice in labeling and organizing their notes. Similarly, if you are teaching students how to form a habit in greeting adults, set up several practice opportunities by asking staff members to pass your students in the hallway as they walk to recess, lunch, the rest room and other locations around the school building. Since individual students learn to manage habits at different rates, plan how to give them more practice than others and to do it without calling attention to the difficulties they're having.

Another aspect in learning how to manage habits is knowing when to use them. Develop this understanding by keeping performance conditions fairly consistent at the beginning of instruction until they learn to associate habits with specific environmental cues and situations. When students practice patterned responses under conditions that are uniform and predictable, they establish a connection between habits they are developing and circumstances under which they use them. For example, when starting to teach a habit in doing long division, limit the type of problems you give and use the same format and symbol to denote the operation. Once you see the cues for long division triggering a consistent patterned response, you can alter the format of the operation, mix in other types of problems or show how to adapt the habit to working story problems.

Sometimes you may need to highlight cues that are subtle or hard for students to focus on, by doing such things as clapping your hands, using highlighting markers, underlining key phases, giving out note cards or showing students how to signal one another. Use extra cues like these to call attention to the natural cues students should use to identify proper times and circumstances for their habits. It's helpful to highlight natural cues when students need to learn to limit their use of habits to a narrowly defined set of circumstances. For example, add extra cues to help students recognize that personalized phrases and mannerisms to greet friends might not be acceptable for greeting adults or classmates, or to learn that strategies they use to remember spelling words may not work well for social studies or science facts. In circumstances like these, use extra cues to show students how to distinguish the characteristics of a friend from those of teachers and other classmates or to differentiate among subject areas for a particular strategy. Students can use these unique attributes as mechanisms to trigger their use of habits.

Habits are not as ritualistic as they seem at first, and students must become skilled at adjusting them to changes in performance demands. As stated, students form habits when tasks are repetitive and routine and when they can use the same patterned response. But even routine tasks change from day-to-day to some degree whether due to the content of lessons, participants in a group, level of difficulty of a task or other conditions. As you continue teaching students to manage habits, vary the tasks and practice opportunities so students learn to adapt and expand performance patterns to fit a wider array of circumstances. Most students will naturally make adjustments in their habits as long as they continue to be successful, but be prepared to help individual students make adaptations when the need arises.

Teaching Students to Overcome Poor Habits

In their attempts at being successful, students sometimes form poor habits that cause them to do tasks incorrectly or inefficiently, disrupt the behavior of the group or create other difficulties for themselves or others. Poor habits may involve following an incorrect performance sequence or adding unnecessary steps to an otherwise correct sequence. They can also include off-task behaviors, mannerisms and other counter-productive responses that bring about negative attention.

Examples of poor habits:

— guessing at answers, rather than thinking them through or working them out,

— complaining or "whining" whenever you ask them to do something,

— talking out in class,

— starting assignments without reading or listening to directions,

— getting up to sharpen a pencil when you pass out a worksheet,

— pushing or shoving when someone touches them,

— playing with hair, pencil or other objects,

— slouching, fidgeting or rocking back in seats,

— swearing, or using distinctive phrases or mannerisms while talking with someone,

— rushing to the next activity or to the front of the line instead of waiting their turn,

— acting defensively any time you correct them or give feedback,

> **"Poor habits are triggered by environmental cues. Sometimes the connection between the cue and the habit is too strong for students to overcome on their own."**

— not looking at or listening to the person to whom they are speaking.

What distinguishes poor habits like these from things students do out of ignorance, forgetfulness or awkwardness is that they're not once-and-a-while occurrences. Rather, they happen so often and under such clearly defined conditions that you can predict when they will take place

Students form poor habits in the same manner they build good habits, and use them in much the same way without thinking about their behavior and the circumstances they are in. In order to change a poor habit, students must first become aware they have the habit and then deliberately replace it with a more appropriate or effective response. Calling student attention to a poor habit is often the quickest and most straightforward approach to teach how to manage it, especially when the habit is not too firmly entrenched. When they realize they're saying or doing something ineffective and that it brings negative attention, they may be able to change the behavior themselves. For example, encourage students who start assignments without listening to or reading directions, to replace this habit with one of acting more attentively by comparing the outcomes of the poor habit with the effective response. Showing them video clips of their behavior, having them self-record the times they repeat a particular action, giving them a model or rubric to follow are some other ways of alerting students to poor habits and their outcomes. If students are unsure what proper replacement behavior is — such as in particular social situations — point out the benefits of observing and imitating the behavior of successful students.

Poor habits, are triggered by environmental cues. And sometimes the connection between the cue and the habit is too strong for students to overcome on their own. You can help students break this connection by masking or blocking out the cues that trigger the poor habit. Once the link is broken, students find it easier to replace the habit and you will have a chance to show them how to do it. For example, if you have students who go to the pencil sharpener whenever you pass out an assignment, give them sharpened pencils along with the worksheets. A few days of dis-associating worksheets with their sharpening of pencils are enough to get them to change their behavior. Similarly, if your students are in the habit of yelling out answers rather than waiting to be called on, have them write down their answers for a few days. Breaking the link between your asking questions and students yelling answers may provide enough of a change to establish the replacement response.

Breaking the connection between a poor habit and the environmental trigger also provides an opportunity to teach students proper habits when they are unable to develop these alternatives on their own. To do this, follow the process described earlier in the chapter. For example, if you have a student who is in the habit of arguing or fighting with a classmate, keep the students separated for a few days. Use this period of separation, when the student is less

"Students form poor habits in the same manner they build good habits, and use them in much the same way without thinking about their behavior and the circumstances they are in."

emotionally charged, to teach positive replacement habits for interacting, such as exchanging greetings, or seeking adult assistance when disagreements arise. To establish positive habits like these, structure several closely-spaced practice opportunities, build a patterned response, and set in place an environmental cue. This approach shows the student how to manage the poor habit by replacing it with one that effectively responds to the situation.

Showing Students How to Form Their Own Habits

Learning to build habits and use them in everyday activities and interactions produces many benefits for students beyond completing tasks you assign. Habits add to the efficiency, ease and self-reliance of most routine things students do whether in school, at home or in the neighborhood. You're limited in the number and types of habits you can teach directly to students, so it's important for them to learn to form habits on their own. The ability to manage habits will enable them to profit from the wide variety of opportunities that arise for them to develop patterned responses suited to their personal needs and characteristics. Your aim, then, in teaching students to manage habits should be not only to improve their performance of teacher-defined tasks, but also to show them how to harness this process in forming their own habits.

Intuitively, students will often develop their own habits and they do this in a straightforward manner. When they succeed at doing a task, they will naturally repeat it at the next performance opportunity if circumstances are the same as before. At the next performance opportunity, they will again try to repeat the actions that worked and strive for more accuracy and efficiency with actions that didn't.

As additional opportunities arise, they will continue to work toward a response pattern that is successful and that minimizes the time, energy and effort they need to expend. With enough practice, students will use environmental cues to trigger a habit in which actions are precise, fluent and self-directed.

There are many things you can do as a teacher to help students develop habits and improve on ones they already have. Explaining what habits are and demonstrating advantages students gain by using them is one place to begin. In this way, students reflect on what they do to form habits so they can carry them out more deliberately. For example, prepare handouts that show the series of steps students go through with tasks they already knew, to demonstrate the habit-building process. Give board work exercises or discussions in which you and the students work out performance sequences for new tasks you introduce. Follow up activities like these with practice opportunities with partners or in small groups to help the students develop and refine patterned responses.

You can also involve students in the selection of the habits you plan to teach, through class discussions or informal surveys where they tell you about habits

"Habits provide the building blocks of efficient, productive behavior and enable students to develop speed, fluency and consistency of performance."

they want to develop or improve upon. Show them how to identify routine and repetitive tasks and have them examine their in-school and out-of-school routines for circumstances that lend themselves to forming habits. Or show them how to explore the benefits they get from using patterned responses to select tasks where habits add to the speed and efficiency of their behavior.

Examples of tasks for students to select:

— organizing their lockers so they can find supplies and materials more easily,

— joining peer groups so they feel less awkward or intimidated,

— asking someone for a date to increase their chances for success,

— giving oral reports in front of the class so they feel more relaxed,

— structuring homework time so assignments get done more quickly and accurately.

— cleaning their rooms or doing other household tasks so they become less of a chore,

— responding to threats or other types of peer pressure so as to minimize conflicts or avoid losing status in the group,

— interacting with parents or siblings to form closer bonds or to avoid reprimands and confrontations.

The approach you take to teach students to form their own habits is much the same as the procedure described earlier in this chapter and in Chapter 3. With an area of behavior in mind for building a habit, show students how to lay out the sequence of steps for completing a task and how to plan a patterned way of doing it. For example, if students want to develop a habit for assembling materials to take home after school, they might list the following steps to complete:

— review the day's schedule class-by-class at the end of the last period,

— go over the list of homework assignments, upcoming tests and projects,

— decide what needs to be done tonight,

— look over the directions for the night's work,

— set out the supplies, materials and handouts to do the work,

— organize the items in their backpacks to take home.

Show them how to use a list of steps like this in developing their own checklist to understand the step-by-step process in completing tasks, to put the steps in a sequential order and to carry out the steps in a way that lends itself to becoming a patterned response or habit.

Habits come from doing things the same way every time, so another thing students must learn is to use a consistent response when they complete routine tasks, especially when doing them for the first time. For example, encourage them to use the same phrases in greeting classmates or starting conversations, the same outline format when they take notes in class and the same strategy for cleaning their room and doing other household chores. With tasks that are more complicated, like participating in a group discussion, doing a report or using a play strategy, show them how to write out or rehearse individual steps in the performance sequence. They could then use these steps as a framework for planning a consistent response pattern and structuring practice opportunities. Over time as they repeat the same series of actions, their performance will become more fluent and efficient.

You can also show students how to structure practice opportunities during the early stages of learning so they develop a fluent, patterned response. For example, if students are forming a habit in assembling homework supplies at the end of the school day, suggest that they practice the steps after each class period so they quickly build a patterned response. This practice helps them refine their actions and solidify the habit. Moreover, it enables them to establish environmental cues to use as triggers for their behavior so they can judge when to use their habits.

In using habits, students gain access to a variety of outcomes over and above those associated with completing a task or activity, such as finishing it quickly and with less effort, and being more accurate in its completion. Most students come to recognize these benefits and factor them in when generating motivation to do routine and repetitive tasks. When students lack motivation for these tasks, help them generate incentive by highlighting outcomes that stem from forming and using habits in these circumstances. For example, point out benefits of using study habits by showing them how to track such things as improvements in their homework scores. With social interactions, have them reflect on how it's easier for them to talk with classmates and how classmates now are more friendly to them. Chapter 4 describes other procedures to help students manage outcomes that follow from their habits.

Developing habits is an important part of student learning and should be an important component in your teaching of self-discipline. Habits provide the building blocks of efficient, productive behavior and enable students to develop speed, fluency and consistency of performance. In Chapter 8, we will discuss yet another way in which you can extend student self-discipline skills: Teaching them to manage school goals and personal goals.

Chapter 8

Managing School Goals
and Personal Goals

Applying Self-Discipline Skills to Goals

A second way of showing students how to apply the self-discipline skills we have discussed in the book is managing external and personal goals. Much of our focus so far has been on teaching students the skills for achieving the goals we have set for them. As we indicated in Chapter 2, the school-and teacher-based goals we choose for instruction usually center on increasing student academic achievement and social competence and on structuring a well-organized and smooth-running classroom environment. These goals are important to student success in school and, although we select them, we should encourage students to take them on as their own as well. In this chapter, we look at ways to show students how to internalize school- and teacher-set goals and take more ownership and initiative for trying to achieve them.

"Keep in mind that students themselves come to school with their own goals — goals that reflect individual interests, desires and aspirations."

We must realize that in addition to goals we have for students, students come to school with their own set of goals — goals that reflect individual interests, desires and aspirations. Many of our students' personal goals coincide with ones we have for them, but there are others that are completely separate and distinct from ours. Helping students acquire skills for pursuing their own goals have a profound an effect on their school performance, motivation and self-reliance as learning the skills for the goals we select for them. As we explore ways to help students take ownership for externally set goals, we should also consider how to teach them to identify and pursue personal goals as well. In this way, they learn to manage the complete goal setting process and direct self-discipline skills toward attaining school-based and personal goals.

School Goals and Self-Discipline

Successful students internalize the goals their teachers, parents and peers set for them as a natural part of their learning and development. One goal teachers and parents have for students is to earn passing grades. Successful students will work long and hard to achieve this goal. However, most successful students probably started their schooling knowing and caring little about earning passing grades. Rather, they simply did what adults told them to do. Young children typically obey teachers and parents even though they don't understand the reasons for doing things they ask. Preschool and kindergarten children commonly express teacher goals in externalized ways, like saying "Mrs. Wilson wants us to do our work," or "The teacher said you should wait your turn." Over time, successful students come to realize that complying with the expectations and demands of adults produces benefits to them both in the short and long-term, and they begin to internalize these goals and take ownership for achieving them. They learn to work toward teacher- and school-based goals without needing special incentives and rewards, and often without even needing to be told what the goals are or how to achieve them. They participate effectively in school activities and interactions because they understand that this behavior helps them produce outcomes with lasting benefit to them. In terms of self-discipline, these students become true managers of their goals because they have taken ownership for achieving them. When this occurs, our task is to encourage and support their behavior and show them how to achieve efficient, effective goal-achieving performances.

By contrast, students who display problems in self-discipline show little understanding and ownership of teacher and school goals and, as a result, their behavior is less focused and self-directed than that of successful students. Some students don't internalize school goals because they don't understand what these goals are or how to achieve them. A student who convincingly promises to turn in assignments every day might not understand what this entails. Other students don't think of their behavior in terms of externally set goals, or perceive such goals as unimportant or unattainable. They may view teacher goals, like learning to complete work on time, to cooperate with teachers or to follow the rules of playground activities, as arbitrary rules or adult-imposed demands. Moreover, they may associate goals like these with failing grades, detention and other negative outcomes they receive when they are unsuccessful at achieving them. Thus, they don't learn to take ownership of the goals nor recognize long-term rewards and benefits they would gain by trying to attain them. As a result, they don't see their day-to-day actions as having a cumulative affect or feel that trying to achieve teacher-set goals would be of no benefit. Rather, they view their actions only in terms of immediate circumstances and results, such as behavior that helps them avoid difficult assignments or embarrassment over making errors, or as behavior that produces desirable adult or peer attention even if it is negative and punitive. Teaching these students to manage teacher and school goals requires helping them develop the skills to understand and value these goals and take ownership and responsibility for achieving them.

Personal Goals and Self-Discipline

Successful students have personal goals they want to pursue in addition to those set by teachers and other adults. One student might want to find out about things not covered in the textbook, another to learn a new game or sports skill, another to have a girl-or boyfriend, make an athletic team or get an after school job at a car repair shop. Goals like these are usually realistic and represent a accurate self-appraisal of abilities, talents, aspirations and circumstances. Because the goals are personal and self-set, successful students will become skilled at using everyday school experiences to pursue them. They may talk over their interests with teachers and friends to get guidance and direction; look for role models among classmates to emulate; seek information from newspapers, magazines and websites; and apply other strategies. Successful students negotiate between their own goals and those of others. They redirect tasks and activities assigned by teachers to suit their own interests, while maintaining a focus on meeting essential standards of achievement. When given a choice, they do assignments and tasks in ways that incorporate their learning styles and interests. They strive to improve their status in the group or solidify friendships even as they ask questions in class, participate in group discussions and work on projects. They constantly take advantage of the opportunities available to them to further their goals and create additional opportunities when conditions permit.

Students who have difficulty formulating personal goals or lack the skills to pursue them often fail to develop the focus that successful students have. Without self-set goals, these students display behavior that appears haphazard because it's not concentrated on a specific aim or set of outcomes. Since these students are unsure what they are trying to accomplish, they don't take the initiative to seek out tasks or opportunities that would be beneficial to them. They may be willing to do what teachers and peers tell them, but when left to their own devices during recess, study hall or free time, they perform in a seemingly purposeless, aimless manner or simply stand on the sidelines. Other unsuccessful students may be able to set reachable goals but don't know how to work toward achieving them. They may be unable to develop or execute a strategy that leads to a personal goal or generate the motivation needed to overcome setbacks or difficult parts of tasks. For example, a student may have a heartfelt desire to become popular with classmates, but consistently holds back because he doesn't know how to approach them and engage in meaningful interactions. Or the student may be able to overcome bouts of shyness or a fear of embarrassment. Some students set personal goals, but choose ones that are unattainable for them, like being the most popular student in class or the captain of the swim team. The frustration at not being able to achieve the goal, or make substantial progress toward it, may lead to complacency, jealously or belligerency. Finally, some students try to pursue personal goals that are in conflict with teacher-or school-set goals and focus their behavior on things that interfere with or run counter to external goals. In some cases these goals are appropriate but the student's approach to achieving them isn't productive or acceptable, such as the student who seeks to improve his status in the group by talking out, clowning or swearing at the teacher. In other instances, the student's personal goals may be harmful or detrimental, like wanting to be a gang leader or taking revenge on a classmate. Improving self-discipline skills of students like these involves teaching them how to develop and solidify goals that are realistic and productive, to negotiate them with those of teachers and classmates, and to structure effective ways of pursuing them.

Teaching Students to Manage External and Personal Goals

There are many things you can do to teach students to manage goals more effectively. This section discusses several important skill areas for managing goals that you can concentrate on in your lessons. You can focus on them with individual students or with the group and incorporate them in your everyday teaching activities.

Understanding What Goals Are

One of the first considerations in teaching students to manage goals, whether they be teacher-set or personal, is to determine whether they have a basic understanding of what goals are and how they apply to their behavior. To assess this understanding, ask students to give examples of things teachers, classmates, or principals expect of all students in given circumstances, like during math class, in reading groups, on the playground or in the hallway. Show students some of your goals and ask them to explain what the goals mean in their own words, or give examples of student behavior that reflect these goals. Have them describe the behavior of students who are successful in pursuing these goals or show them videos of classmates doing things like turning in homework, engaging in a class discussion, participating in playground games or making friends. Then ask them to identify the goals these behaviors signify. To assess an understanding of personal goals, have students describe things they would like to learn to do or the type of person they would like to become; select a favorite hobby, game or free time activity; or identify a community worker or classmate they admire. You could also prepare an interest inventory or survey geared to your students' background and age level to probe their understanding of goals and aspirations. Information from activities like these, along with other sources — like things the students talk about or show an interest in during unstructured times — help you decide whether you need to begin your teaching with building a basic understanding of what goals are and what they entail.

"Teaching students how to set behavior goals is another important skill in self-discipline because those who have clearly defined goal are better able to direct their actions toward achieving them."

Choosing Goals to Work Toward

Teaching students how to set behavior goals is another important skill in self-discipline because those who have clearly defined goal are better able to direct their actions toward achieving them. You can help your students learn how to select behavior goals as a class lesson or as an individualized teaching activity. One approach is to have students prepare a list of subject matter topics, study skills, games, areas of social interaction and other potential goals they would like to learn, or choose items from a list you develop. Then, have the class designate the areas it would like to work on, or have each student select an individualized set of target goals. For example, begin the school year or a new semester by making a list of things your students would like to learn in your class or other school settings. Go through each content or topic area in your curriculum to assess areas of interest to the group and show students how they can pursue personal interests in the context of instructional lessons. With this information, involve students in planning activities that incorporate their goals in the curriculum and develop lessons on topics of widespread interest. You might also encourage students to include one or more personal goals in their list to reflect specific interests and aspirations. In addition, integrate this goal setting process in your report card grading system. Students could make personalized cards for a grading term based on goals they are working on, grade their progress on the cards and take the reports home for parents to sign. Adapt this approach for individual students who need more instruction in goal setting by having them prepare weekly or bi-weekly report cards targeted on short-term academic, social, personal or study habit goals. In these ways, students learn to choose individual or group goals that are suited to their interests, abilities and learning styles and carry out strategies for pursuing them.

Identifying Attributes of Goals

Once you have assessed student understanding of goals and discovered areas they're interested in achieving, focus teaching on one or two areas that quickly capture their interest and motivation. As much as possible, let students choose goals to work on or encourage them toward ownership in these activities. Sometimes you will find that even with specific aims in mind, students are unaware of the things they have to do to attain certain goals or are unfamiliar with the benefits they can derive from them. In this case, teach them about the attributes of these goals, highlight the behavior of those who are attaining them, and stress the benefits of goal-related achievement. This type of information helps them make more informed decisions about goals and ensures more realistic and attainable selections. For many school goals, such as working on assignments, studying for quizzes and following classroom rules, describe them in a one-on-one situation and explain them in concrete down-to-earth terms, or pair students with classmates who are skillful in demonstrating goal-related behavior. Showing videos, reading short stories, setting up visual displays and using other engaging methods to highlight goal-related behavior are other ways to improve student knowledge of goal-related behavior. In these circumstances, an essential component of your teaching is structuring opportunities in which students are successful in their initial attempts at pursing these goals and immediately derive benefits from their behavior. These approaches help improve student understanding of personal goals, but you may also need to draw broadly from outside resources and structure activities. For example, to help students explore and solidify their own interests, have classmates give demonstrations of various hobbies and games, invite guest speakers, structure a job fair, organize field trips or connect students with community programs.

Making Goals Attainable

Some students understand the notion of goals but are so overwhelmed or confused by the number of things they have to do to pursue them that they give up trying. Showing these students how to subdivide a goal into short-term manageable tasks or objectives can help them see goals as more attainable. For example, students who are daunted by different aspects of earning a passing grade, such as reading chapters, doing board work assignments, completing daily worksheets, passing tests, working on a final project might learn to view earning a passing grade as a reachable goal if they focus on each aspect individually and in a shorter time frame. For example, show them how to develop a grade book or assignment log that helps them track each task separately. If this approach is too challenging, have the students work on just one or two sub-goals that promote ownership and advancement in a key area of behavior. For example, instead of trying to become the most popular student in class, have the student work on becoming a study buddy by providing needed instructional support to a struggling classmate. In this way, the student progresses toward the goal of popularity by earning one classmate's respect and uses this achievement as a stepping stone for increasing status with a wider group. The focus of your teaching should be on showing students that improvement in one or two fundamental areas of behavior can provide the framework for developing other goal-related skills.

Achieving personal goals can also be daunting to students when they have an image of what they would like to accomplish but are unable to set a clear path in that direction. Not knowing where to begin in pursuing personal goals leads students to thinking these goals are unattainable. A student might have a desire to jump rope or play basketball during recess but ends up watching on the sidelines because she is unsure where to start learning the basic moves. Or another student might have an exciting idea for a homework project on space travel but ends up choosing a simpler or less motivating one because of an inability to structure a complicated one. In cases like these, teaching students to view a goal as attainable involves helping them gain a clear picture of the goal so they know where to begin. Sometimes encouraging students to ask for help or giving them time to brainstorm ideas with a classmate is all the help they need. Once they know how to get started with a goal, their motivation and drive may be sufficient to see them through. For complicated goals, show students how to visualize it by teaching them an organizing structure such as a web, a matrix or task analysis that helps them lay out steps in concrete or sequential ways. Similarly, setting up one-on-one or small group practice sessions, or using videotaped demonstrations can be effective methods for showing students how to begin pursing such goals as learning games, asking a classmate for a date or participating in a job interview.

"Teaching students to view a goal as attainable involves helping them gain a clear picture of the goal so they know where to begin."

> **"If you incorporate high-interest topics or games in your instructional lessons, students experience a wider array of benefits from their behavior."**

Structuring Activities for Pursuing Goals

Another skill area to focus on with your teaching is showing students how to structure activities that lead to achieving a goal once they have a specific aim in mind. Teachers have long noted that the more input students have in planning activities, the more motivated and self-directed they become. Moreover, you can often increase student ownership and initiative in pursuing goals by demonstrating that such activities can become productive avenues for utilizing their strengths and talents. Actively involving students in instructional lessons gives them a way to pursue personal interests while progressing toward the goals you set. For example, if you incorporate high-interest topics or games in your instructional lessons, students experience a wider array of benefits from their behavior.

Ways to involve students in structuring activities:

— showing them how to develop their own spelling lists, practice worksheets, story outlines and study guides,

— introducing a new curriculum area or unit and asking them to explore topics and applications they are particularly interested in learning about,

— teaching them how to choose materials, instructional aids and other learning resources suited to their interests, talents, learning styles and preferences,

— having them invite guest speakers with whom they can discuss history or science topics,

— having them videotape models that demonstrate job interviewing techniques, employee etiquette or other employment skills,

— designing teaching units around their personal experiences, such as tracing their ancestry, writing autobiographies or researching background information on their hobbies or sports heroes,

— scheduling special interest days during which they plan lessons, monitor activities and evaluate learning outcomes,

— having them keep journals to reflect upon how daily school activities relate to their career goals or personal interests,

— having daily or weekly discussions on how mathematics or science topics apply to their everyday life experiences.

Tracking Progress in Attaining Goals

Teaching students how to evaluate progress toward attaining goals is another area you can address in your teaching. Self-recording and -monitoring of goal-related behavior allows them to see first hand the advancements they are making in skill development. One important aspect of having students assess their progress is showing them how to define goals in measurable terms so they can identify the various behaviors or tasks they involve. Another is helping them set benchmarks for measuring goal-related behavior which they can track on a chart, graph, log or other means.

Ways to help students develop a framework for evaluating progress:

— showing students how to grade their math worksheets, spelling quizzes, sports performance or interactions with classmates,

— giving them check sheets for tallying their progress in learning games, reading works of literature or learning topics of personal interest,

— having individual conferences with you so together they can co-evaluate the stories they write or projects they complete,

— having them videotape class presentations so they can review their public speaking strengths and set targets for improvement,

— setting up learning centers and other classroom areas that encourage alternative ways for learning geography, history or job skills,

— having them set deadlines for completing science or art projects and showing them how to develop rubrics for grading such tasks,

— negotiating contracts with them that have mutually agreed upon aims, timelines and outcomes for such areas as making friends or turning in homework.

Using approaches like these to encourage students to take an objective, firsthand look at their behavior promotes greater responsibility for attaining goals.

Students who learn to use their self-discipline skills to pursue external and personal goals are well on their way to becoming true managers of their behavior. You will see them starting to internalize school- and teacher-set goals and assume more ownership and initiative for trying to achieve them. There will be less of a need for you to give students special incentives, rewards or other inducements to work toward school goals because they will more clearly understand that goal-directed behavior has personal and lasting benefit to them. These skills will enable students to formulate and pursue their own goals as well. As students come to see their classrooms and school as places where they can achieve aims that interest them, they gain a stake in helping to create settings and activities that are safe, productive and beneficial to themselves and to the school community as a whole.

Appendix

Examples of Possible Goals Matched to Individual Student Problem Behaviors

PROBLEM BEHAVIOR	POSSIBLE GOALS
Aggressive behavior, e.g., hitting, kicking, throwing objects, tattling, swearing, tormenting peers	• Learn to show consideration for others • Learn to display acts of courtesy • Learn to share toys and supplies • Learn to wait turn in activities • Learn to exchange greetings with peers and to talk about age appropriate topics • Learn to show anger or frustration in age appropriate ways
Overt disruptive behavior, e.g., excessive talking, making distracting noises, wandering around the room, showing preoccupation with objects	• Learn to ask permission before leaving assigned area • Learn to work without distracting others • Learn to select proper times and situations to have conversations • Learn to assemble and organize material before beginning activities • Learn to ask teacher or classmates for help when needed • Learn to follow the rules for games or other activities • Learn to plan out sub-tasks for doing an assignment and to monitor progress in work
Noncompliance, e.g., refusing to stop an activity or to start the next one, acting defensive or argumentative, making excuses for not doing as told	• Learn to follow rules and routines of the classroom, lunchroom, hallways, etc. • Learn to carry out the directions of teachers • Learn to review directions for assignments and activities before starting them • Learn to identify the benefits and outcomes for following rules and directions • Learn to discuss and negotiate rules for games before beginning play • Learn to make choices or to choose alternative ways of doing tasks
Tantrums, e.g., pouting, screaming, kicking out, pounding objects, stomping feet, rolling around on the floor	• Learn to express frustrations in an age appropriate manner • Learn to state preferences and desires • Learn to negotiate differences of opinion • Learn to suggest alternatives to the directions and demands of others • Learn to delay gratification of wishes and desires • Learn to follow the rules for using playground equipment or play objects • Learn to accept apologies from others

PROBLEM BEHAVIOR	POSSIBLE GOALS
Impulsive behavior, e.g., starting activities before reading or listening to directions, acting without considering the effects, responding without forethought	• Learn to read directions before beginning assignments • Learn to formulate or rehearse questions and answers before raising hand • Learn to check answers against the directions that were given • Learn to wait one's turn during a game or other activity • Learn to begin making comments by re-phrasing or summarizing what some else said • Learn to use stock phrases when greeting someone or joining a peer group
Inattention, e.g., fidgeting, wiggling, daydreaming, playing with small objects	• Learn to recognize when activities are about to begin • Learn to begin tasks at the same time as classmates • Learn to observe and follow the lead of students around them • Learn to complete assignments in a timely manner • Learn to use written directions or checklists to guide and track performance • Learn to follow a consistent pattern or routine in performing tasks • Learn to re-direct behavior to the task at hand
Sullenness, e.g., being lethargic or unresponsive, acting without a sense of purpose or initiative, showing a generally low energy level	• Learn to display good posture, show animation and use conventional mannerisms • Learn to exchange greetings with teachers and peers • Learn to initiate activities and interactions with classmates • Learn to respond to the comments of others • Learn to participate in games and recess activities • Learn to engage in playful teasing • Learn to track and monitor (or grade) work on assignments • Learn to celebrate one's successes and accomplishments
Repetitive behavior, e.g., hand flapping, hopping, spinning, rocking, screeching, scratching and showing other self-stimulatory or injurious behavior	• Learn to follow a routine in performing tasks or assignments • Learn to express interests, needs and desires • Learn to occupy free time in constructive ways • Learn to make choices and decisions about behavior • Learn to play with toys and participate in games • Learn to follow the directions of teachers • Learn to tell others when finished with tasks • Learn to interact cooperatively with peers • Learn to ask teachers or neighbors for help when needed • Learn to use materials and resources to complete tasks

PROBLEM BEHAVIOR	POSSIBLE GOALS